Christopher White
has been Director of the Ashmolean Museum,
and Fellow of Worcester College, Oxford since 1985. He
began his career in the Department of Prints and Drawings at
the British Museum, London, and has since held the posts of
Curator of Graphic Arts at the National Gallery of Art,
Washington (1971–73) and Director of Studies at the Paul
Mellon Centre for Studies in British Art (1973–85). He has
written widely on Dutch art, particularly on Rembrandt, and
is also the author of books on Rubens, Durer and English
landscape. His catalogue of the Dutch pictures in the
Royal Collection was published in 1982.

# WORLD OF ART

This famous series
provides the widest available
range of illustrated books on art in all its aspects.
If you would like to receive a complete list
of titles in print please write to:
THAMES AND HUDSON
30 Bloomsbury Street, London WC1B 3QP
In the United States please write to:
THAMES AND HUDSON INC.
500 Fifth Avenue, New York, New York 10110

Printed in Singapore

CHRISTOPHER WHITE

# Rembrandt

with 171 illustrations, 16 in color

THAMES AND HUDSON

*To Rosemary*

*Frontispiece*: Self-portrait at the age of thirty-four
(detail), 1640

© 1984 Thames and Hudson Ltd, London

First published in the United States of America in 1984 by
Thames and Hudson Inc., 500 Fifth Avenue, New York,
New York 10110
Reprinted 1995

Library of Congress Catalog Card Number 83-51330
ISBN 0-500-20195-1

Printed and bound in Singapore

# Contents

## Preface

Exactly twenty years ago I wrote a biography entitled *Rembrandt and his World*, long since out of print, in which I attempted through a precise account of the artist's life and ambiance to offer a more truthful portrait than emerges from the romantic interpretations which the artist regularly attracts. Apart from revising my text to bring it up to date with recent scholarship, which involved substantial rewriting in a number of places, I have taken the opportunity to expand the scope of the original book by including a discussion of Rembrandt's art as well as his life with the intention of providing a more comprehensive introduction to the artist.

It is greatly to be regretted that the present owner of what is arguably Rembrandt's greatest portrait, that of *Jan Six*, has refused permission for it to be reproduced in this book.

## CHAPTER ONE

## A provincial youth

'20 MAI 1620 REMBRANDUS HERMANNI LEYDENSIS STUDIOS [US] LITTERARUM
ANNOR[UM] 14 APUD PARENTES.' This brief notice of Rembrandt's
registration as a student at the University in Leiden is the very first
reference to the artist. It is no more cryptic than the various documents
referring to any great man's early years, but in Rembrandt's case the
situation remains much the same throughout his life. We have almost
exclusively bare facts with no gloss: legal documents, church notices of
baptisms and burials, and records of purchases of both property and works
of art. With few exceptions they tell us no more than the events they
record, and like Shakespeare's 'laundry bill' depend on our interpretation.

Literary sources are fortunately a little more illuminating, although
Rembrandt's own 'literary remains' amount to no more than seven
business letters, formal and dignified in tone, in which the writer never
allows his personality to emerge. Contemporary accounts of his life and art
are frequently positively misleading. Rembrandt never had a Condivi, nor
would he have wanted one. Perhaps he got the biographers he deserved;
certainly none of them put his point of view.

The two principal seventeenth-century biographies, both published
after Rembrandt's death, were written by the German artist and writer

1 Notice of Rembrandt's registration as a student, 1620

2 PIETER BAST *View of Leiden* (detail), 1601

Joachim von Sandrart (1675) and by the Italian writer on art, Filippo
Baldinucci (1686). The former had worked in Amsterdam from 1637 until
the early 1640s, and would therefore have known the artist and his practice
up to this time. On the other hand he wrote from a classicist point of view,
which rendered much of Rembrandt's art unsympathetic and deplorable.
The Italian writer was entirely dependent on the testimony of a former
pupil of Rembrandt, Bernhard Keil, who had left Amsterdam by 1651.
Apart from the attitudes of the two writers, neither could speak with
authority on the last twenty-five to thirty years of the artist's life. The
longest and most circumstantial life, written by the Dutch writer Arnold
Houbraken, only appeared in 1718. Although as a pupil of Samuel van
Hoogstraten, in turn a pupil of Rembrandt, he had direct access to first-
hand knowledge, he wrote at a time when a combination of a classicist
critique inimical to the late Rembrandt in particular and a mass of legend
had developed. Yet although much of the criticism in these and other
writings on the artist is often based on false premises and inaccurate
information, enough of value remains to piece together with the known
facts a reasonably rounded image of the artist.

Turning to Rembrandt's art one soon discovers that no one has treated
the human emotions more directly or more profoundly. 'One should be
guided only by Nature and no other rules,' he is supposed to have said – and
by and large he practised what he preached. He surrounds us with living,
thinking people and invites us to converse with them, to share their joys
and sorrows. They are so real that it is tempting to assume that they are an
elaborate self-portrait and that his art is directly dependent on the events
and emotions of his own life. But between the two there is often a wide

8

gap. The detachment that any artist shows towards his daily existence is no less present in the work of Rembrandt, though it is more deceptively camouflaged.

The personality of the painter is elusive. From the numerous self-portraits he stares thoughtfully and directly, but with a great sense of withdrawal. He is watching as much as he is being watched. He does not yield up his secrets easily. He has all the reticence of a true Dutchman.

Rembrandt Harmenszoon van Rijn was born in Leiden on 15 July 1606, the son of Harmen Gerritszoon van Rijn and Neeltge van Suydtbroek. The date of his birth is significant, for only three years later Holland was to achieve the peace and freedom for which she had been fighting so doggedly. The Twelve Years Truce was Spain's recognition of her independence. From war, the country was able to turn to more creative cultural and economic aims. It seems hardly fortuitous that Rembrandt's life should span the most fertile period in Dutch history.

3 PIETER BAST *Bird's eye view of Leiden* (detail), 1600

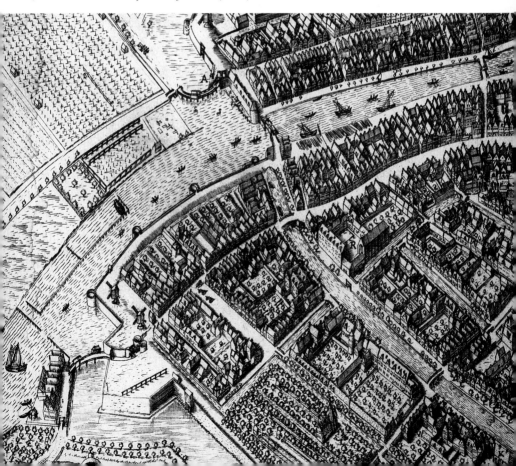

The town where Rembrandt was born was, thanks to its position at the centre of the cloth industry, rich and powerful in the seventeenth century, second in size only to Amsterdam. With the Old Rhine as a border on one side, Leiden was built along a wide canal, called the Rapenburg. Today it retains its essential character and allows us to sense the elegance and stateliness which was once part of its daily life. Above all, it boasted a famous university which attracted foreigners from all parts of the world. No other Dutch university approached it either in size or standards. Its pride was pardonable.

Rembrandt's family connections with the city of Leiden go back to 1513, when his great-great-grandfather is mentioned as a miller there. In 1575, his paternal grandmother and her second husband, a miller, bought a windmill outside the town. She and her two children by her first marriage, Rembrandt's father and aunt, had already joined the miller in one of the

3  houses he owned in the Weddesteeg, a small street on the north of the town near the Wittepoort. The houses overlooked the Rhine, and their view of the constant flow of river traffic was framed on both sides by windmills, one of which was owned by the family, and was later called De Rijn.

The two children remained in their mother's new home until the daughter left to marry a bargee. A few years later the son, Harmen, also married, choosing Neeltje van Suydtbroek, a baker's daughter, as his bride. Harmen moved, but not far. Shortly after his marriage he concluded a deal with his stepfather whereby, for a specified sum, he bought half of the windmill in the Weddesteeg (no. 1 on the map), part of the building adjoining it, and a newly built house (no. 2) adjoining his stepfather's (no. 3). He also called himself Vande Rijn after his mill. It was probably in this house that Rembrandt was born, the last but one in a family of at least nine children. His father belonged to the Reformed Church, in which Rembrandt was brought up, while his mother continued to practise as a Roman Catholic, a fact indicative of the general religious tolerance to be found in Holland.

Rembrandt, who tended to take his models from those around him, may well have left us a number of studies of both parents. The most plausible likeness of his father occurs in a drawing inscribed with the sitter's name in

4  a contemporary hand. Style confirms what common sense tells us. It cannot have been made long before his father's death in 1630. The expression on the face shows the old miller oblivious to the outside world, and totally absorbed in clinging to his fast-departing strength. Indeed it has been suggested that this drawing provides evidence that Rembrandt's father went blind in old age, which, if true, would give a personal reason for the artist's later partiality for themes connected with blindness.

4 *The Artist's Father(?), c.* 1630

The artist's mother, who outlived her husband by ten years, may have been a more frequent model at least up to the time of her son's final departure from their home town. A later inventory gives her as the subject of an etching, but there can be no certain identification between her and the old woman who makes frequent appearances as the personification of dignified old age in various guises in a number of Rembrandt's early works. One example of the latter was presented to Charles I shortly after it was painted, but apart from the fact that the model is arguably a good deal older than the artist's mother would have been at the time, it was catalogued within a decade of its execution as a genre study rather than a portrait. (A self-portrait, also in Charles I's collection, was accurately described.)

5

11

*5 Old Woman: the Artist's Mother(?), c. 1629*

No doubt Rembrandt's brothers and sisters played their part as models but none of them can be identified with any degree of certainty in his work, although some attempts have been made to recognize his eldest brother, Adriaen, who spent the whole of his life in Leiden, first as a shoemaker and then in the family business of milling. Like Adriaen the remainder of the family stayed in Leiden and the men probably became tradesmen. After his final departure for Amsterdam, Rembrandt appears to have had almost no further contact with his family.

Rembrandt must have stood out as the intelligent member of the family, for at the age of seven he was sent to the Latin School where, as the name suggests, he would have been well grounded in Latin, as well as religious instruction of the Bible from the Calvinist viewpoint. From there he entered the University seven years later. Though it must have been fairly unusual for a miller's son to go to university we cannot credit Rembrandt's parents with clairvoyance. He was a clever boy and they took advantage of the education available, which also gave him a number of privileges, such as exemption from civic guard duty and a tax-free quota of wine and beer. But it took Rembrandt only a few months to make up his mind that he was not suited to academic learning and to persuade his parents to remove him. Though far from being the illiterate that some of his biographers made him out to be, Rembrandt does not appear to have been wholly in sympathy with Dutch humanistic learning. The allegorical and emblematic literature of the time was largely alien to his art. But when the occasion arose, he was perfectly capable of looking up a Classical text and understanding the spirit of what he read.

His parents allowed him to take up painting, which by this time must have emerged as his presiding passion. They apprenticed him to Jacob van Swanenburgh, an undistinguished local painter of portraits, architectural scenes and *diableries* in the manner of Hieronymus Bosch, who had been to Italy, returning with a knowledge of the Italian scene and a Neapolitan wife. Rembrandt spent three years in his studio, where he must have learnt the mechanics of painting, if little more. No reflection of his first master can be discerned in his earliest works.

For all its importance as a centre of learning and trade, artistically Leiden was a backwater. In 1624 the more important part of Rembrandt's artistic education began. He was sent to Amsterdam to work for six months in the studio of Pieter Lastman, who after a year or two in Italy working under the influence of both Caravaggio and Adam Elsheimer, had set up as a successful and influential painter of religious and mythological subjects. Rembrandt's second master, unlike his first, made a deep impression on him. His work for the next few years shows his debt, and some ten years

6 PIETER LASTMAN *The Angel and the Prophet Balaam*, 1622

later he was still making copies after paintings by Lastman. It was in his studio that Rembrandt developed the taste for Biblical subjects which remained with him for the rest of his life, unlike other Dutch painters of the century. Moreover, he learnt from Lastman's example to depict them in dramatic compositions enhanced by a wide range of lively expressions and gestures in bright clear colours.

By 1625 Rembrandt had returned to Leiden and set up as an independent artist. He can have felt little challenge from the local painters who, apart from his former master, Van Swanenburgh, consisted of such minor figures as Joris van Schooten, a painter of still lives and the occasional Biblical subject. It was then if not before that he came into contact with his fellow townsman Jan Lievens, one year his junior. According to the account of the local burgomaster, Lievens had been apprenticed to Van Schooten at the age of eight (Rembrandt was still at his Latin School), and two years later went to work in Lastman's studio in Amsterdam. He is then reported to have returned to Leiden after a further two years and set up as an independent painter at the unlikely age of twelve in 1619. What he looked like about a decade later can probably be seen from a supposed self-

7 Jan Lievens *Self-portrait, c.* 1635

portrait, possibly painted in England, which contains more than a touch of the Van Dyckian elegance that was to lure him away from the style of his Leiden years. It is a revealing facet of Lievens' character that his conceit and refusal to accept criticism was remarked upon by both Constantijn Huygens shortly before this picture was painted, and by the aging Earl of Ancrum living in retirement in Amsterdam twenty-five years later.

When Rembrandt returned to Leiden he was nineteen and Lievens eighteen. Perhaps Lastman suggested that Rembrandt call upon his old pupil. Their common training gave them a unity of purpose which shows in the similarity of their aims during these years, and within a few years their works were being confused. An inventory of paintings belonging to Prince Frederick Henry in 1632 refers to 'A Simeon in the Temple, holding Christ in his arms, done either by Rembrandt or Jan Lievens'. The local historian said that they shared a studio, which is quite likely.

14

8      Rembrandt's appearance at this time can be seen in an etching, though he was probably using himself as a model rather than producing an intentional self-portrait. It has all the spontaneity of a vigorous pen sketch, which was no mean achievement on a grounded copper plate, even if it cannot be regarded as a technical success. There is something aggressive and slightly farouche about the coarse-featured face. The large bulbous nose which in so many later self-portraits Rembrandt took pains to hide is here quite apparent. The hair is wild. But it is the eyes with their piercing intensity which give stature to an otherwise uncouth appearance. Awkward and uncompromising he undoubtedly was; the determination which never allowed him to swerve from his own chosen path is already apparent in his face.

A very different impression is gained from a painting executed about the
9      same time, which unlike the etching probably was intended as a self-portrait. Painting with an unusual degree of finesse for the Leiden years, the artist presents himself in the most flattering light. Carefully arranged shading softens the effect of the plebeian nose, and the beautifully groomed hair and kiss-curl add a touch of surprising elegance. He is stylishly if fancifully dressed in a gorget over a white collar. With its cool, aloof expression, the portrait must have been designed to impress. Probably a more accurate record of Rembrandt's appearance can be gathered from the
10     picture painted by his companion, Jan Lievens, about the same time. The sitter's aspect is pleasant and honest but considerably less aristocratic. The beret, curled hair falling over the scarf tied around the neck, also protected by a gorget, offer more than a hint of the young artist.

Rembrandt lost no time in establishing the pattern of his artistic career, and most of his recognizable characteristics are already to be seen in embryo in the works he produced over the next six years. Unlike the majority of his fellow artists in Holland, he never allowed himself to become a specialist in one or two areas. Although we revere him above all as an interpreter of religious subjects and as a portraitist (an aspect of his work only to be developed in his Amsterdam years), during the course of his life he turned his attention at one time or another to mythological and Classical subjects, landscapes, nudes, genre scenes and even the occasional still life, although he never appears to have produced a flower-piece. And within each category of subject he often crosses the border to another, so that genre will be subtly merged with portraiture, portraiture with religious iconography, religious iconography with landscape, and so on. His range of expression provides evidence of a unified artistic personality rather than merely suggesting an adept exponent in different areas of specialization.

16

8 *Self-portrait Bareheaded*, 1629

9 *Self-portrait, c.* 1631

Variety was a factor in every aspect of his art. At one moment he works on a miniature scale in an exquisitely refined technique, at the next on a monumental size with a bold and broad execution of brush or pen. The tradition of the 'peintre-graveur' had already been established in the sixteenth century by such artists as Dürer and Mantegna, but Rembrandt was to realize the potentialities of a double career in an entirely novel manner. He painted, drew and etched from the outset, although to begin with the first was the prime medium and the other two followed in its wake. But he soon learnt to develop both drawing and etching along paths of their own, and to attain the inherent pictorial possibilities of each medium. Moreover, as an added refinement we discover that certain subjects tend to be explored in one medium rather than another. Possibly the most original aspect of his practice as an artist is to be found in his attitude to drawing. In the Renaissance it was conceived as a preparatory means towards achieving the finished work in whatever medium. The apotheosis of this tradition is reached in the work of Rubens, most of whose

18

10 JAN LIEVENS
*Portrait of Rembrandt, c. 1628*

drawings were executed with an ulterior purpose. With Rembrandt only a small percentage of his drawn oeuvre can be classed as working studies for paintings or etchings. For the most part he used drawing either to record what his eye saw or to create the images in his imagination, and as a few contemporary collectors already acknowledged the results stood as self-contained works of art.

The two artists did not work unnoticed for long. Already in 1628 when a jurist from Utrecht, a certain Aernout van Buchell, visited Leiden he wrote in his notebook, 'The Leiden miller's son is greatly praised, but before his time.' The man from Utrecht was not so ready as the artist's townsmen to see genius writ large. Van Buchell was right in the end, but was it for the right reasons?

A different kind of tribute to Rembrandt's popularity is his acceptance in the same year of his first pupil, Gerrit Dou, then a boy of fourteen, who probably stayed in the master's studio until Rembrandt left for Amsterdam. Dou, however, remained behind in Leiden to become the founder of the Leiden school of 'fine painters' and one of the most successful and fashionable artists of the age. His pupilage established a practice which continued throughout Rembrandt's life. By the time he left Leiden for Amsterdam, he probably already had three other pupils working under him. His popularity as a teacher expanded immeasurably after his move and Sandrart in his biography makes a special point of saying that he 'filled his house in Amsterdam with almost countless distinguished children for instruction and learning'. Even in later years when his popularity among fashionable society had waned he was not to work alone in his studio.

In the story of Rembrandt's recognition by his contemporaries, a no less important event took place in 1629, and credit for this must undoubtedly go to Rembrandt's friend, Jan Lievens. By the winter of 1626–7 Lievens' name had reached the ears of Constantijn Huygens, Secretary to the Prince of Orange, who commissioned a portrait from the young Leiden painter. There was some criticism among Huygens' friends but the patron was satisfied; 'some people are of the opinion that the thoughtful expression does not give a true portrait of my character. But at the time I was seriously preoccupied with important family matters, and my eyes reflected the cares of my heart.' On 6 April 1627 Huygens was married.

For a young artist Huygens was the right person to know. He had a distinguished and highly successful career as a diplomat and courtier. He was ten years older than Rembrandt and had started his career as Secretary to the Dutch Embassy, first in Venice and then in London, where he was knighted by James I. In 1625 he was appointed Secretary to the Stadholder, Prince Frederick Henry of Orange, and remained in the service of the House of Orange until his death over sixty years later.

Apart from his career, he was a dilettante of wide interests and accomplishments. He kept a detailed diary, wrote an autobiography, and carried on a correspondence with Descartes in three languages. He wrote Latin verses, as well as finding time to translate the poetry of John Donne into Dutch. He was an accomplished player of the chitarrone. He studied astronomy, theology, and jurisprudence, and he was sufficiently athletic to climb the spire of Strasbourg Cathedral. But above all he was passionately interested in the visual arts. He would have become an artist had not his father forbidden him. Painting was to be encouraged as one of the liberal arts, but not as a full-time occupation. The artist *manqué* had to rest content with his activities as artistic adviser to the Stadholder.

In 1629 this polyglot and virtuoso visited Leiden. He did not fail to call on the young man who had painted the portrait, and one assumes that at the same time he made the acquaintance of Rembrandt. For Rembrandt

11 JAN LIEVENS *Constantijn Huygens* (detail), 1626–7

this was an important moment, while on his side Huygens was impressed, and made much of it in his autobiography. He was fully aware of the humbleness of their origins. For him this convincingly disproved the theory of the superiority of noble blood, an argument frequently aired in the aristocratic milieu of the writer. He judged Rembrandt and Lievens as already the equals of the most famous painters (this just a year after Van Buchell's crabbed scepticism), and forecast that they would soon surpass them.

Huygens found both Rembrandt and Lievens both unconcernedly self-absorbed in their own restricted world and was clearly puzzled why they refused to visit Italy. For the North, Rome had become the Mecca of art, and from the second half of the sixteenth century onwards an increasing number of artists had flocked there, sometimes to remain for the rest of their lives. It was a sign of the times that Huygens should ask Rembrandt and Lievens why they did not make the pilgrimage which would have given them the opportunity of studying the art of Michelangelo and Raphael. The young men, who, it must be remembered, were trained in the studio of an artist who had spent a year or two in Italy, answered that they were far too busy in the flower of their youth, and besides, some of the finest Italian works were to be seen in Holland. This joint reply has a ring of independence and practical truth, which from subsequent events we know to be more characteristic of Rembrandt than of Lievens, even if one cannot go as far as to identify the former as the spokesman. Throughout his life Rembrandt lived up to his word and made drawings after Italian and other works which were absorbed into the bloodstream of his art.

Huygens, apart from making intelligent conversation, studied and criticized their work. Lievens' had a grandeur of invention and boldness not to be found to such a marked degree in the work of Rembrandt. But the latter was superior in judgment and the representation of lively emotional expression. Huygens picks out Rembrandt's *Judas returning the Thirty Pieces of Silver*, painted in this year, to prove his point. He praises the description of the differing emotions of each of the participants, above all the agonized remorse of Judas. In a small panel Rembrandt has conjured up a dramatic scene from the Bible. This is the first acknowledgment of the supreme storyteller Rembrandt was to become.

Huygens may well have turned his admiration into something more immediately concrete. The same year the Earl of Ancrum visited the Netherlands as Charles I's personal representative, to offer his master's condolences to the King and Queen of Bohemia on the death of their son. Frederick Henry presented Ancrum with a painting by Lievens, which he in turn gave to Charles I. Probably at the same time he took back two paintings by Rembrandt, a self-portrait and the study of an old woman (his mother ?), which were also presented to Charles I. Ancrum would have met Huygens by virtue of his position, and they would have found one another congenial company, for Ancrum was a lifelong friend of John Donne, whose poems Huygens had translated. Perhaps Huygens recommended Rembrandt as an artist worthy of representation in the English royal collection either directly to Ancrum or more probably to the Stadholder who included them with a painting by Lievens as part of the gift.

During his years in Leiden Rembrandt's art developed rapidly from such Lastman-inspired works as *The Angel and the Prophet Balaam*, painted the year after his return from Amsterdam, in this instance probably in direct emulation of his former master's treatment of the same subject. The highly

22

12 *The Angel and the Prophet Balaam, 1626*

expressive gesticulating figures of the two participants, painted on a grand scale in cool contrasting colours, fill the foreground of the picture and actively engage the spectator's attention in the vigorous if unsubtle drama which unfolds. But already we see something of Rembrandt's originality in his emphatic description of each figure in bold brushstrokes, as well as his transformation of the horizontal format invariably used by Lastman to a vertical, allowing Rembrandt as yet unrealized opportunities to depict an airy atmospheric space. He was soon to introduce the latter quality into his work by the use of chiaroscuro. Modified and refined over the years, it became one of his most powerful vehicles of expression. At first employed as a highly successful pictorial device, it was gradually moulded into an immensely subtle means of suggesting psychological insight. The source for this unusual play of contrasts between light and shadow was in its initial form the painting of Caravaggio, known to Rembrandt to some extent from Lastman's work, but which he could have seen more deliberately imitated in the works of the Utrecht artists, Gerrit van Honthorst and Hendrick Terbruggen. A little later Rubens' adaptation was to provide yet another example.

The effect of the introduction of chiaroscuro in Rembrandt's painting is immediately visible in *Judas returning the Thirty Pieces of Silver*, and to a

13 *Judas returning the Thirty Pieces of Silver*, 1629

14 *The Presentation in the Temple*, 1631

greater extent in *The Presentation in the Temple* of two years later. In the
latter work, the artist has fashioned a spot of brilliance over the huddled
central group within a darkened interior, so that mysteriously he discloses
the vast vaulted building peopled with chance spectators. By placing the
main action further back than he did in his earlier works, the artist draws
the viewer into the scene, determined at its nearest point by the two elderly
figures, who sit in the foreground like a Greek chorus witnessing an event.
Conveyed by delicate brushwork, atmosphere, that most intangible of visual phenomena, has now become an essential feature of Rembrandt's art.

15 CORNELIS DANCKERTS Map of Amsterdam, 1654

16 REINIER NOOMS, called ZEEMAN *The Rokin with the Exchange in the Background, Amsterdam*

## CHAPTER TWO

## Amsterdam and prosperity

After their initial success both Rembrandt and Lievens must have soon realized that Leiden was too small an artistic centre to provide them with the scope and commissions they needed and felt entitled to. And to prove the point, the first major commission came to Rembrandt from Amsterdam in 1631, when he was required to portray the rich merchant, Nicolaes Ruts (The Frick Collection, New York). Lievens on the other hand is recorded in the same year as having gone to England for several years to undertake work for the English court. It marked the end of a memorable and original partnership. Henceforth the lives and progress of the two artists diverge. Lievens pursued a more fashionable course, largely inspired by Flemish painting, which he studied first-hand in Antwerp on his way back from England, while Rembrandt took what was eventually to become a much more solitary path.

Amsterdam around 1630 was at the beginning of its heyday. It was a prosperous, rapidly growing city of about 150,000 inhabitants. From being much like any other town in Holland, it had suddenly captured from Antwerp the position of the leading port of northern Europe. It impressed all who saw it. In later years Fénelon described it under the disguise of Tyre 'crowded with merchants of every nation and its inhabitants are themselves the most eminent merchants in the world. It appears at first not to be the city of any particular people but to be common to all as the centre of their commerce. The vessels in this harbour are so numerous, as almost to hide the water in which they float; and the masts look at a distance like a forest.' Descartes, less romantically, complained that 'everyone is so engrossed in furthering their own interests that I could spend the whole of my life there without being noticed by a soul'.

Besides reaching a position as a leading mercantile city, it was also becoming a centre of learning and culture. From a provincial town, it was changing into the economic and cultural capital it has since remained. In 1632 the Athenaeum Illustre was founded and later became the nucleus of the new university. The previous year Casparus Barlaeus, a Remonstrant theologian from Leiden, arrived and was appointed Professor of Philosophy and Medicine, to be followed in turn by other famous men.

What must have impressed Rembrandt above all was the rapid new building trying to keep pace with economic expansion. Already what had been fields beyond the city when Rembrandt was last there was now built over. The plan of the three main canals or *grachten*, which is the basis of the modern city, was still being carried out. The leading architect of the period was Hendrick de Keyser, who designed in the characteristic Dutch style: red-brick houses with sandstone decoration and elaborate gables. In the year that *The Anatomy Lesson of Professor Tulp* was painted, the Westerkerk and the New Lutheran Church designed by him were completed. By the end of the decade the city had its first theatre. Vondel could write, for once without exaggeration, that 'here resided the soul of the State of Holland', or, expressing it in an international context, of 'Amsterdam which wears the crown of Europe'.

In the field of painting Amsterdam may have lacked the solid establishment and originality of the school of Haarlem or the special character of what was being produced in Utrecht, but it offered a more

17 Thomas de Keyser *The Anatomy Lesson of Dr Sebastian Egbertsz.*, 1619

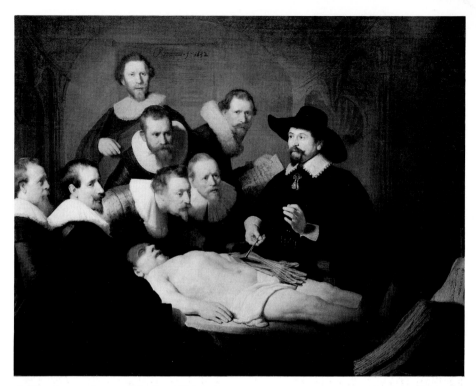

18 *The Anatomy Lesson of Professor Tulp*, 1632

flourishing scene than Leiden. History painting was still represented by Lastman, who with the brothers Pynas, Jan (died 1631) and Jacob, produced religious and mythological subjects in the manner of Elsheimer. In the field of portraiture the favour of the Amsterdam clientele had been captured by the precise, sober, unemphatic images of its leading citizens painted by Nicolaes Eliasz. and Thomas de Keyser, respectively fifteen and ten years older than Rembrandt. With a good supporting cast already in action, there was a vacant role for a star, which Rembrandt lost no time in assuming.

Rembrandt's *pièce de réception* was *The Anatomy Lesson of Professor Tulp*, finished in 1632. The tradition for this kind of group portrait went back to the previous century. Dissections were few and far between – this was only Tulp's second – and they were treated as festive occasions attended by large crowds. Rembrandt effected a revolution in the manner of representation. Earlier examples had amounted to little more than a series of posed portraits arranged around a skeleton, skull or head. Thomas de Keyser's

17 commemoration of *The Anatomy Lesson of Dr Sebastian Egbertsz*. in 1619 had sought to introduce some movement and variety by giving self-conscious gestures to the two groups of men ranged on either side of the skeleton. It was a group portrait first and foremost, with only the skull providing a symbol of the nature of the event. Rembrandt transformed his group portrait into a 'history piece'. Instead of the posed group of standing figures, he shows us the dissection in progress, or so it would seem. (It has also been suggested that the picture records a private dissection among colleagues which took place either immediately before or after the public occasion.) Eager surgeons cluster round the professor, who starts his dissection with a discussion of the left hand, taking his authority from the book propped up at the corpse's feet. (Tulp regarded himself in the direct tradition of Vesalius, and we can surmise he follows the relevant plate and text in the great anatomist's epoch-making book of anatomy.) Rapt inner unity is created as the praelector speaks and acts and his audience look and listen. The active motions of the mind are eloquently conveyed in contrast to the inertia of the corpse, placed in such a conspicuous diagonal position. But if we are led to believe we are witnessing an actual event, we are deceived, since the dissection invariably began with the stomach and not the hand. Although presented with the trappings of reality, the picture was not intended as an accurate record of what took place, and was as much symbolic of the occasion as Thomas de Keyser's picture of thirteen years earlier. What impresses us and, we may deduce, Rembrandt's contemporaries is that the picture offers a living symbol of a particular event.

Although probably commissioned by Tulp and paid for by those portrayed, the painting belonged to the Amsterdam Guild of Surgeons, 19 which from 1619 to 1639 had a temporary anatomy theatre somewhere on the upper floor of the south tower of the Anthoniesmarkt, which is seen in an etching by Zeeman. The old gateway on the left has been transformed into a weighhouse. Later on they moved to St Margaret's Hall, but by the end of the century the Guild and the pictures were once again installed in the Anthoniesmarkt.

By a nice stroke of irony, the victim, who as usual was a criminal, was also a native of Leiden who had been hanged for robbery with violence. The hero of the piece, however, was one of the most distinguished members of the Amsterdam establishment. Nicolaas Pietersz., or as he called himself, Tulp, was the son of a cloth merchant. In 1619 he built himself a splendid house on the Keizersgracht, near the Westerkerk, which had a tulip sculpted on the gable stone, and eleven years later built another 132 for his son-in-law, Arnold Tholinx, who was to be portrayed in one of

30

19 REINIER NOOMS, called ZEEMAN *The Anthoniesmarkt, Amsterdam*

Rembrandt's finest etchings. In 1628 Tulp was appointed lecturer in anatomy to the Amsterdam guild of surgeons, with the title of Professor, and delivered his first public lectures in January 1631. In addition he found time to be a magistrate, Curator of both the Latin School and the University, and to hold office eight times as City Treasurer and twice as Burgomaster. He was a scholar of repute, and a member of the Muiden circle. His artistic tastes were narrow, and he was a religious bigot, but he was useful to know, and it can hardly have been coincidence that the medical profession were among the most faithful of Rembrandt's patrons throughout his life.

In March 1631 Rembrandt had bought 'a well situated garden lying outside the White Gate' at Leiden, suggesting that he had no intention of moving. But he must have suddenly changed his mind and took up residence in Amsterdam sometime after the beginning of July that year, because as his first biographer, J. Orlers of Leiden (1641), explained, his art met with such favour among the citizens of Amsterdam that he received numerous commissions for portraits and other works. What may have been intended as a relatively short visit became a lifelong stay, so that Rembrandt remained in Amsterdam for the rest of his life. Apart from a few journeys in Holland, nearly all undertaken for some specific purpose,

31

he hardly travelled at all, and never as far as we know left his native country. Unlike Lievens, what he told Huygens was the truth. He was too busy to travel.

Four drawings of English views, two of Old St Paul's, London, one of Windsor Castle, and another of St Alban's Abbey, have sometimes been taken as proof that Rembrandt visited England in 1640, the year in which two of them are dated. None of the four is topographically accurate, and all show a considerable amount of fantasy. It is very unlikely that the artist saw the scenes with his own eyes and the drawings were probably based on views made by another artist. Around 1640, both several years before and after, the same kind of architecture appears in the background of a number of Rembrandt's paintings. It was probably in connection with these that Rembrandt made four variations on a theme of English medieval architecture.

More inexplicable is George Vertue's remark that Rembrandt visited Hull in 1661–2 and made a number of portraits of seafaring men. Though there is no evidence to render this sea journey impossible, nothing we know of the artist and his work gives a shred of confirmation to this surprising statement. Vertue was writing nearly fifty years after the artist's death, and was relying on the testimony of someone who was only a boy of nine at the time of the supposed journey.

On 26 July 1632, a notary, acting on behalf of a tontine set up in Leiden, called at an address in the Breestraat, where he was told that Rembrandt was living. He was made to wait in the hall while a serving-girl went to fetch him. When Rembrandt appeared, the notary with nice legal precision first checked that he was indeed talking to the artist, and then remarked that he 'found him still fresh-faced, robust and mentally alert'. He took his leave, his mission accomplished.

Although insignificant in itself, this event establishes that Rembrandt was living in the house of an art dealer called Hendrick van Ulenborch, who was twenty years his senior. Rembrandt already knew him when he was still living in Leiden. The artist had lent him the not insubstantial sum of one thousand guilders, an indication of how much he was earning by this time. Clearly they became friends and partners, and both professionally and personally the dealer was to be a major influence in Rembrandt's life.

Van Ulenborch had spent much of his youth in Poland, where his father was cabinet-maker to the king. After a spell as a painter in Denmark he set up as an art dealer in Amsterdam in 1627. He quickly established a thriving international business, which included the importation of Italian pictures and involved numerous partners as well as artists. One of his smaller operations was to act as publisher for one of Rembrandt's largest etchings.

20 *A Bearded Old Man*, 1634

He was a Mennonite and well connected with the community, who purchased a part share in the business. As a result Rembrandt, apart from learning about a religion which was to have considerable relevance to his art, was provided with a number of profitable introductions to wealthy patrons. The art business came to a sad end after Van Ulenborch's death, when his son was accused of selling fakes to the Elector of Brandenburgh and fled to England, where he was appointed 'Purveyor and Keeper' of Charles II's pictures.

Van Ulenborch was also to establish, possibly with Rembrandt's assistance, what Baldinucci called 'La famosa Accademia di Eulenborg'.

This was a kind of art school for the children of good families who learned to paint by copying pictures. Quite incidentally, Van Ulenborch would sell the copies. His house must have become a centre where people interested in art could meet. It must have been a congenial place for the young artist from Leiden, and gave him wider contacts. In the summer of 1634 a German from Weimar, Burchard Grossmann the Younger, made a journey through Holland carrying his autograph album with him. He either knew or had an introduction to Van Ulenborch, and he visited him. Van Ulenborch inscribed a highly appropriate motto for a successful dealer, 'In restraint lies strength'. Rembrandt was introduced and invited to contribute. He wrote 'an upright soul respects honour before wealth', put his signature, and then drew the head of a bearded old man with hands clasped together on the opposite page.

But the most important person Rembrandt met in Van Ulenborch's house was the dealer's young first cousin from Friesland, Saskia van Ulenborch. She was the daughter of a former Burgomaster of Leeuwarden, where she was born on 2 August 1612. Her father, whose death left her an orphan at the age of twelve, was a remarkable man of considerable means, who had studied law at Louvain and then practised as a lawyer. He quickly came to the fore and performed various duties such as Pensionary and Burgomaster for his native city and for Friesland. Sent on a political mission to William the Silent in The Hague, he was invited to dinner and had the disquieting experience of witnessing his host's assassination. Shortly afterwards he was a member of the delegation sent to Elizabeth I to plead for sovereignty of the Netherlands.

When Saskia, the youngest of her family, was about ten, she was sent to stay in Amsterdam, probably with one of her much older Van Ulenborch cousins, either Hendrick or more likely Aaltje, married to Jan Cornelis Sylvius, who acted as her guardian. She must very soon have met Rembrandt, and what happened next is most eloquently told in a drawing, underneath which the artist wrote: 'This is drawn after my wife, when she was 21 years old, the third day after we were betrothed (i.e. exchanged betrothal vows) – 8 June 1633'. To emphasize the preciousness of the occasion Rembrandt has used silverpoint on prepared paper, a method employed by the early Renaissance and later used for portrait drawings by Goltzius and De Gheyn. Saskia holds a flower in her hand and gazes intently at her fiancé while he sketches her. On her head she wears a large straw hat with a band of flowers. Only the unromantic refuse to believe that Rembrandt chose her hat for this intimate occasion, and there is already an indication of the Flora she was to become. This exquisite and intimate study, recalling Dürer's 'Mein Agnes', must have meant more in

21 *Saskia in a Straw Hat*, 1633

*22 Jan Cornelis Sylvius, 1634*

plighting their troth than any formal document. This is truly a lover's drawing.

Almost exactly a year later to the very day, Rembrandt and Saskia's guardian appeared before the Commissioners in Amsterdam to take part in a ceremony similar to that of calling the banns. For Rembrandt there is a proviso that his mother's consent must be obtained, and a marginal note tells us that later she in fact appeared before the notary in Leiden and gave her consent to the marriage of 'the honourable Mr Rembrandt Harmensz van Ryn'. He was the only son to whom she gave the courtesy title 'Mr'.

Saskia's guardian, Jan Cornelis Sylvius, was a preacher who, after a number of country posts in Friesland, where he had met his wife, had settled in Amsterdam and officiated at the Groote Kerk. It was only appropriate that Rembrandt should portray him, and this he did in the same year in an etching. Sylvius sits in an ecclesiastical interior, looking dignified, sober, and humane, with his hands resting on a Bible.

He remained a close family friend. He stood in as witness at the baptism of the first child, and performed the ceremony for the second. Several years after his death, Rembrandt did another etching and a painting of him.

By his marriage, Rembrandt had made a move up in the social scale. Saskia's family belonged to the prosperous upper class. Of her three brothers, two were lawyers and one was an army officer. One sister was married to a professor of theology, and another to a commissioner.

The fourth sister, Hiskje, was married to Gerrit van Loo, who was the Town Clerk of Het Bilt, a polder in Friesland. It was probably in order that the marriage could take place from their house that Rembrandt and Saskia were married on 22 June in the Reformed Church of Sint-Annaparochie, the chief town of Het Bilt. Rembrandt had joined Saskia in Friesland a few days after the ceremony in Amsterdam. In the marriage contract Saskia was described as living at Franeker, so she probably spent her last days of maidenhood at the house of her recently deceased sister, who had been married to the Professor of Theology there.

They were soon back in Amsterdam, where they lived with her cousin Hendrick van Ulenborch for the next two years. Their happiness is shown by the number of times Saskia appears in Rembrandt's work. His eyes follow her everywhere. She is an unconscious model in a drawing showing her asleep in bed, one hand resting on her breast, the other on the coverlet. Rembrandt's pillow can be seen behind her. Although their marriage was to end tragically early, all the evidence points to a harmonious union. They were undoubtedly happy in their natural extravagance.

In the year of their marriage Rembrandt painted Saskia as Flora. Her hair is decked with flowers and she holds a staff entwined with leaves. Her

23

24

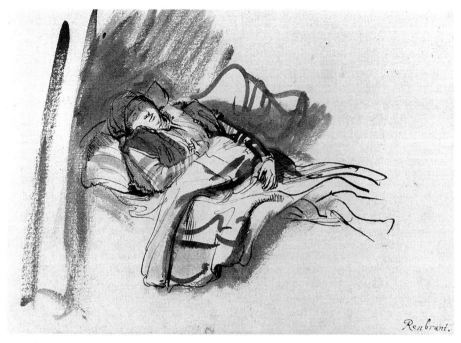

23 *Saskia Asleep in Bed, c.* 1635

clothes are oriental in their richness. Rembrandt used them on several occasions and they formed part of the artist's studio accoutrements, to be produced for any suitable occasion. She is walking through a landscape of rich vegetation, like a stately priestess on her way to sacrifice in some pantheistic rite. She stops to turn and look at us, holding up her bulky cloak before her. There could be no more enchanting goddess of Spring. In these years pastoral poetry and painting were the fashion, followed by Rembrandt, who found it suited his purpose in his exploration of costume pieces, which can be interpreted as an offshoot of his current absorption in painting 'history pictures'. The picture clearly pleased him so much that he produced another variation in the following year (National Gallery).

25 Two very different images of the artist and his wife are due more to artistic intention than variation in life-style. In the picture, probably painted about 1635, Saskia, wearing a heavy green dress, sits on the artist's knee and looks back at us over her shoulder. Her expression is decidedly dignified and is in marked contrast to that of her husband, whose coarse

24 *Saskia as Flora*, 1634

25 *Self-portrait with Saskia, c.* 1635

26 *Self-portrait with Saskia*, 1636

ebullient features are wreathed in a grin. He wears a fur hat with an enormous white feather, and holds up a glass of wine to drink the health of the spectator and boast of his possession. He might be some bravo boasting of a conquest from a painting by Caravaggio or one of his northern followers. A feast, including a peacock, a symbol of pride and *luxuria*, is set out on the table, and a tally board hangs on the wall behind. There is reason to suppose that in this work Rembrandt intended a moralizing subject such as the Prodigal Son in the tavern, in which following the convention of the time he used identifiable models. For a more deliberate image of the artist at home one must turn to an etching of 1636, in which the couple are shown seated soberly at a table while he draws.

As so often in those days, the history of their children would reduce a modern mother to despair. Of the four born to Saskia, only the last, Titus, survived to grow up. Rumbartus, the first, was baptized in the middle of

27 *Saskia with One of her Children, c.* 1637

December 1635; he lived for two months. He was followed by two daughters, both called Cornelia. The first was baptized in July 1638, and was buried three weeks later. The second was baptized in July 1640, and lived only two weeks. Among the very many studies of the 1630s, a large proportion are of women and children. The artist Jan van de Cappelle possessed a portfolio of drawings by Rembrandt entitled 'The Life of Women'. Many show children rather than babies; they must have been studied from families other than his own and indicate the detached artist looking for models. One, however, may well show Saskia with one of her children, either Rumbartus or Cornelia I. It is drawn in black chalk in that wonderful fluent shorthand which Rembrandt developed for his studies in these years. The mother sits up in bed nursing her baby, who lies contentedly in her arms.

Shortly after Rumbartus' birth, Rembrandt and Saskia left Van Ulenborch's house. In a letter to Huygens written in 1636, Rembrandt says: 'I am living next door to the pensionary Boreel, Nieuw Doelenstraat.' Willem Boreel was a lawyer attached to the East India Company and lived beside the Kloveniersdoelen, where *The Night Watch* was to hang. The street runs along the side of the Amstel away from the Munt Tower. The houses lived in by Boreel and Rembrandt must have been brand new, since building only began on the site in the previous year. Rembrandt's house was two beyond the one seen on the extreme right in an eighteenth-century drawing of the street; the building which stands back from the road is the Kloveniersdoelen.

28 R. VINCKELES *The Doelenstraat, Amsterdam*

One of Rembrandt's first tasks as husband was to travel to Rotterdam and give power of attorney to Saskia's brother-in-law, Gerrit van Loo, so that he might collect outstanding debts to his wife and claim interest on her money. Before his marriage Rembrandt was clearly not hard up, as both his loan to Hendrick van Ulenborch and the numerous commissions he received make abundantly clear. Saskia certainly brought him some additional wealth, though it should be remembered that her father's estate had to be divided among eight children. Although Sandrart specifically says that 'he was not a spendthrift', the evidence points to the contrary, and Rembrandt must have spent much of what he earned. Baldinucci describes the artist as often going 'to sales by auction; and here he acquired clothes that were old-fashioned and disused as long as they struck him as bizarre and picturesque, and those, even though at times they were downright dirty, he hung on the walls of his studio among the beautiful curiosities which he also took pleasure in possessing, such as every kind of old and modern arms – arrows, halberds, daggers, sabres, knives and so on, and innumerable quantities of exquisite drawings, engravings, and medals, and every other thing which he thought a painter might ever need'. His name appears frequently as a buyer of works of art at auction sales during these years. On one such occasion he acquired a painting of *Hero and Leander* by Rubens. But his purchases did not pass unnoticed by Saskia's family. When a family row broke out over the estate of Saskia's parents, one member accused Saskia of spending her inheritance in 'a flaunting and ostentatious manner'. This charge was vigorously refuted by Rembrandt and Saskia, who claimed that 'they were abundantly blessed with riches'. (Rembrandt never forgave them and years later when Titus, aged fourteen, made a will, a clause was introduced that explicitly excluded any relatives on his mother's side from receiving any part of the inheritance.)

Rembrandt's fame as an artist grew rapidly, and commissions for portraits poured in from every quarter. One result of his popularity was the number of pupils who sought to be taken on. It was during these years that Ferdinand Bol, Jacob Backer, Govaert Flinck and Gerbrand van den Eeckhout, his favourite, who, according to Houbraken, became one of his closest friends, all worked in his studio. They were later to capture their master's popularity with fashionable clientele. Houbraken says that in order to accommodate all his pupils, Rembrandt took a warehouse on the Bloemgracht, where he partitioned the room so that each pupil could work by himself. It was there that one pupil and a model were supposed to have undressed. They had no sooner proclaimed their similarity to Adam and Eve than the master, whose attention had been drawn by the curiosity of the other pupils, drove them from the house with the words 'but because you are naked you must get out of Paradise'.

It is apparent that his pupils, apart from working on their own, were employed on making copies of their master's pictures. From 1637 onwards there are numerous references in inventories and sales of such copies in collections or on the market. One collection belonging to a painter and an art dealer associated with Van Ulenborch contained one original and no less than six copies after Rembrandt, clearly listed as such. Given the perennial concern for establishing the extent of Rembrandt's oeuvre, it is a fact that should be borne in mind.

*The Anatomy Lesson of Professor Tulp* was undoubtedly a success. Tulp himself may well have recommended Rembrandt's services to his many influential friends and he was fast becoming the fashionable portrait painter of Amsterdam. How far Rembrandt was on social terms with his sitters is another matter, and one on which there is almost no evidence. In his present euphoric mood it is difficult to believe he would have rejected any overtures, and his marriage to Saskia certainly gave him the entrée to a number of houses.

Among the more fashionable sitters were Marten Soolmans and his wife 31, 32 Oepjen Coppit, who were painted in 1634. Soolmans was the son of a refugee from Antwerp, who studied for a few years without much success in Leiden. But in 1633 he married Oepjen Coppit, who was a member of one of Amsterdam's most distinguished families. From then until his death in 1641 his comfort was assured. They lived close by Rembrandt.

The artist portrays them full length on separate canvases though he contrived them as a pair. Soolmans holds out his hand with his glove loosely held by the fingers in a somewhat casual gesture towards his wife. The stately figure of Oepjen Coppit moves towards her husband, though she turns to give us a penetrating if reserved glance. They are depicted against a grand but simple setting. It is the kind of portrait that Frans Hals was doing so well, but here Rembrandt has introduced a touch of Vandyckian *hauteur*. He has allowed himself to be carried away in painting the rich clothes, rosettes on the shoes, belts, lace collars and cuffs. But, unlike the Flemish master who made the clothes the servants of the sitter, Rembrandt's faces are a little dull and smooth in comparison to the richness of the accessories. In such works we see Rembrandt adapting a style of portraiture in character more with a court than a republican community, although this may well have expressed the aspirations of some of the patrician members of Amsterdam society.

A more original solution posed by the problem of the double portrait had been completed in the previous year in *The Shipbuilder and his Wife* (Jan

Rijcksen and Griet Jans), in which the husband is represented at work surrounded by the appropriate tools of his profession, either designing a ship, or, it has been suggested, working on an illustrated treatise on shipbuilding. Dividers in hand he looks round as he is interrupted by his wife bursting in to his cosy study with a letter for him, suitably bearing his name and address. The missive is made both the formal and psychological focus of the composition. The split-second timing of this domestic event is emphasized in the way that the wife keeps hold of the door handle. And as if reflecting the different nature of the commission – a master shipbuilder

30 THOMAS DE KEYSER *Constantijn Huygens with his Clerk(?)*, 1627

29 *The Shipbuilder and his Wife*, 1633

was not the social equal of a wealthy burger – Rembrandt has executed the heads and hands in more open brushwork, which can be studied as it creates form and colour, stroke upon stroke, vividly suggesting the living tissues beneath the outer skin.

As a means of creating a focus in a double portrait, the letter motif had already been used, for example, by Thomas de Keyser six years earlier in his portrait of *Constantijn Huygens with his Clerk* (?), but without the sense of urgency and concentration through which Rembrandt transformed a portrait into a genre scene. This picture represents one of the first occasions

31 *Marten Soolmans*, 1634

when the artist seeking a more informative portrait represents the sitter in action in his daily professional life. It was a method which Rembrandt was to turn to notably good account in a number of his portrait etchings.

Rembrandt was especially at home among the professional classes, particularly the Church and Medicine, which throughout his life provided 33 him with commissions. In 1635 he made an etched portrait of the Arminian Remonstrant preacher Jan Uytenbogaert, then an old man of nearly eighty, but who in his time had been very influential. He had been called to The Hague by Prince Maurice and Oldenbarnevelt and was tutor to Prince Frederick Henry. He was chief spokesman of his sect in their struggle with the Calvinists and was exiled for his pains. After a few years in Paris he finally returned to Holland in 1626 but never recaptured his former influential position. He became preacher at the Remonstrant Church and it is as such, surrounded by his books in an atmosphere of scholarly calm, that Rembrandt portrayed him. A poem by Hugo Grotius inscribed below may

32 *Oepjen Coppit*, 1634

possibly indicate that Rembrandt was acquainted with the distinguished statesman, jurist and author.

One of Rembrandt's friends who belonged to quite another religion was the Portuguese Jewish author, Menasseh ben Israel. He lived in the Breestraat, which Rembrandt had temporarily left, and was Rabbi at the synagogue just round the corner from Van Ulenborch's house. He was one of the most distinguished of the Jewish community, who taught Spinoza and was the first Hebraic printer in Holland. The etched portrait 34 Rembrandt made of him in 1636 was far less elaborately worked up than that of Uytenbogaert and this may reflect a more informal commission.

Throughout his life he remained a friend of the artist. Before his departure for England on a mission to Cromwell to plead for the recall of the Jews, from which he never returned alive, he published a book entitled *The Illustrious Stone, or the Statue of Nebuchadnezzar. . . .* The book is a mystical work based on the author's view of the Second Advent. He

33 *Jan Uytenbogaert,*
*the Preacher,* 1635

34 *Samuel Menasseh ben Israel,* 1636

35 *Cornelis Claesz. Anslo*, 1640

commissioned his old friend to make four illustrations, one showing the image seen by Nebuchadnezzar in a dream, which had a head of gold and feet of clay and was destroyed by a stone. Although the combination of etching and drypoint used for this work was unsuited for mass reproduction in a book, the patron was clearly satisfied with the result,

36 *Herman Doomer*, 1640

since the copy presented to the dedicatee, Isaac Vossius, is one of the few to contain Rembrandt's illustrations.

Cornelis Claesz. Anslo, a Mennonite preacher and theological scholar, also active as a cloth-merchant, was another sitter who was probably also a friend. He belonged to the more liberal group of his community, the so-called Waterlanders, and took a leading part in the acrimonious discussions between the various Baptist sects. In 1641 Rembrandt etched his portrait and painted a double portrait of the preacher and his wife in which concerted action, seen in the *Shipbuilder and his Wife*, presented a unified image. In the preparatory drawing for the painting he is shown seated in a chair, a massive imposing figure, in the act of expounding some belief, with his literary authority, the Bible, at his side.

Calvinist intolerance of other religions, particularly the Remonstrants, had greatly increased after the Synod of Dort in 1618, but by the time Rembrandt was living in Amsterdam other beliefs were practised, although not always free from attacks of religious bigotry, made more complicated by the entanglement of religion with politics. Rembrandt, a true liberal, limited his circle to no one sect, as these portraits of sitters of different religions make clear. His liberality was not, however, the result of indifference. In his own unorthodox way he was a deeply religious man, but it is doubtful whether he followed any one religion. His attitude can be most closely matched by that of the Mennonites, whose creed is based on the original and literal content of the Bible and excludes all dogmas based on subsequent events. (Baldinucci in fact goes so far as to call him a Mennonite.) Their preference for 'the poor in spirit' to 'the worldly wise and learned' might be Rembrandt's own motto, and the emphasis on inward reaction rather than outward manifestation could stand as his artistic credo of later years.

Rembrandt's sitters were drawn from all ranks of society. From the artisan class were Herman Doomer and his wife, painted on commission in 1640. Doomer, a countryman from across the German border, had established himself in Amsterdam as an ebony worker and a furniture and frame maker, and may have acted in the last capacity for Rembrandt. Their honest simplicity could not be more eloquently expressed in their portraits. The husband wears a simple jacket with an unostentatious lace collar. His hat is tipped back a little on his head and he almost blinks at us as if our gaze was like a light that shines too strongly. His wife, with firmly clasped hands, is equally unostentatious. They had six children, one of whom, Lambert, was probably a pupil in the master's studio at the very time he was painting the parents. The portraits were greatly prized possessions. When the wife died, a widow, she left them to Lambert, on the sole

35

condition that he have them copied for each of his brothers and sisters.

Considered as studies of human physiognomy rather than records of social standing, Rembrandt's portraits reveal a fundamental change between his earliest examples done at the beginning of the decade and a work such as *Herman Doomer*. The outward rendering of the appearance skilfully if superficially realized in *Marten Soolmans* was abandoned in favour of an inner portrayal which was increasingly to determine Rembrandt's treatment of the face, whether in a portrait or in an imaginary subject. That he was able to do this was largely due to his brilliant mastery of chiaroscuro and application of paint. The pattern of shadows was broken up so that instead of the simple contrast between one half of the face in light and the other in shadow, light and shadow alternate in numerous small areas of varying intensity over the entire face. Above all, the most subtle gradations of shadow are applied to the area around the eyes, which in the later portraits immediately capture the attention, and lead the spectator on with the sensation that through the eyes can be read the mind of the person represented. Rembrandt's sitters tend to become increasingly introspective and withdrawn, and indulge in the minimum of movement and expression. Everything is concentrated on the gaze rather than the surface description of the face, which is now suggested by the handling of the brush, ranging from almost tangible impasto to the most translucent glazes, expressed in a combination of sympathetic rather than contrasting colours. No longer does the brush follow outline and form in its movements, but freely creates a soft blurred image of the person enveloped in the atmosphere of the setting. To acquire a harmonizing element, the previously plain backgrounds become interesting in themselves and are constantly varied in shape, colour and above all chiaroscuro. The entire surface of the picture is skilfully devised as a background to the portrayal of a thinking human being.

The sitters described so far may have been friends as well as patrons. But the one person above all during the 1630s who claims the role of chief benefactor – if not exactly a patron, then as *éminence grise* – is Constantijn Huygens. His interest in Rembrandt when he visited him in Leiden was no passing phase. It can hardly have been chance that in 1632 Rembrandt was asked to paint a pair of small panel portraits, done in a miniature-like technique, of Constantijn's elder brother, Maurits, Secretary to the Council of State in The Hague, and of a close family friend, Jacob de Gheyn III, the artist, who later became a Canon of St Mary's at Utrecht.

Undoubtedly, Huygens' most direct influence was on Frederick Henry of Nassau, Prince of Orange, Stadholder of Holland. He was born in Delft in 1584 and had been tutored by the Arminian Minister, Jan Uytenbogaert,

31

37 P. PONTIUS *Frederick Henry, Prince of Orange* (detail), 1628

whom Rembrandt portrayed in an etching many years after this event. Court taste was strongly orientated in favour of Flemish art, particularly Rubens and Van Dyck, and it is hardly suprising that Frederick Henry had himself painted by Van Dyck, a picture which was made widely known through the engraving. In contrast to the rather thin introspective young man who appeared in an earlier portrait, Van Dyck has given him the proportions and self-confidence of a ruler.

In 1632, in what was probably Rembrandt's first commission from the Stadholder, he painted the latter's wife, Amalia van Solms, bust length, half in profile in a painted oval decorative frame as a pendant to a similar portrait of her husband executed in the previous year by the fashionable international artist Gerrit van Honthorst. It must have been seen as a compliment that the young Rembrandt should have been paired with the latter, who had acquired fame and standing by his work for Charles I. Moreover, it gave Rembrandt the opportunity of a sitter in a different class from his Amsterdam clientele. Compared with the superficial glazed

38

image of husband dressed in armour, presented in profile, Amalia van Solms appears less idealized and more in the sober manner of Rembrandt's bourgeois portraiture. That the two pictures did not hang together has been interpreted as a sign of dissatisfaction with Rembrandt's production, and it is a fact that he was never commissioned to paint another portrait by the Stadholder.

Whatever his views about portraiture, Frederick Henry, in spite of the Flemish bias to his taste, clearly felt drawn to the art of Rembrandt. The year the Prince succeeded his father Rembrandt began his career in Leiden. The incidents connected with the acquisition of two paintings by Rembrandt which the Earl of Ancrum took to England have already been 14 mentioned. So has the painting *Simeon in the Temple holding the Infant Christ in his Arms* by Rembrandt or Jan Lievens, described in the 1632 inventory of the Prince's possessions. The work in question is possibly one of two paintings of this subject by Rembrandt, with the odds marginally in favour of the version of 1631. (One if not two early representations of the subject by Lievens might equally well qualify.)

Rembrandt's major work for the Stadholder was five paintings of subjects taken from the Passion, a commission which through his habitual reluctance to finish occupied the artist throughout the 1630s. (It is possible that an earlier painting of the *Crucifixion* of 1631, now in a small country church in France, may have had some connection with the series, if no more than to demonstrate to the court of what the artist was capable in the field of religious painting.) During this time Frederick Henry was engaged in decorating his various residences, and Rembrandt's paintings were probably intended to adorn the Noordeinde Palace in the Old Court in The Hague. It was in connection with this work that the artist wrote seven letters to Huygens, asking for his help and his intercession. This correspondence makes one suspect that Huygens not only supervised the work but was also directly responsible for getting Rembrandt the commission. If he was, it would not have been the first time that he recommended an artist to his master. In any case he took an intense interest in how matters progressed, and insisted that all Rembrandt's paintings be first sent to his house for him to inspect, before he passed them on to the Prince himself.

40 *The Descent from the Cross* is one of the two pictures finished in 1633. It is Rembrandt's tribute to Rubens. This fact cannot have been lost on the Stadholder, and may well have affected his decision to ask Rembrandt to carry out the remaining paintings for him. (Only six years before, the Flemish artist had visited Holland, though there is no reason to believe that he ever met Rembrandt.) The composition of Rembrandt's picture echoes

38 *Amalia van Solms, 1632*

Rubens' famous painting in Antwerp Cathedral, which Rembrandt would have known through Vorsterman's engraving. On this occasion Rembrandt followed the Flemish practice of reproducing the picture in a print fully protected by a privilege granted by the States General, and published by his host at that time, Hendrick van Ulenborch.

Rembrandt writes to Huygens, probably in February 1636, that 'I am very diligently engaged in completing as quickly as possible the three Passion pictures which His Excellency himself commissioned me to do . . . one has been completed, namely Christ ascending to heaven, and the other two are more than half done.' A few weeks later Rembrandt writes again to say that he is sending the finished *Ascension*, and that 'I shall follow anon [i.e. to The Hague] to see how the picture accords with the rest. . . . It will show to the best advantage in the Gallery of His Excellency since there is a strong light there.'

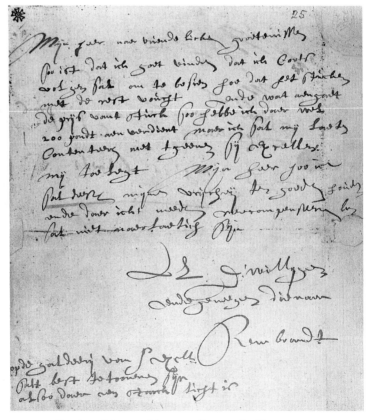

39 Rembrandt's second letter to Constantijn Huygens, 1636

40 *The Descent from the Cross*, 1633

There is silence for three years, but this does not necessarily mean that there was no contact between the two men. In February 1638 a tournament and other festivities were organized by Huygens in The Hague to celebrate the marriage of the sister of Amalia van Solms, Princess of Orange. Rembrandt may have been present – an invitation would have been no 56    more than his due – and the group of drawings of Negro bands and mummers on horseback could date from this occasion.

At last on 12 January 1639 the artist could write to Huygens that 'because of the great zeal and devotion which I exercised in executing well the two pictures which His Highness commissioned me to make [*The Entombment* 41    and *The Resurrection*] . . . these same two pictures have now been finished through serious application.' He asks 'whether it would please my lord that the two pictures should first be delivered at your house as was done on the previous occasion. . . . And as my lord has been troubled in these matters for the second time, a piece 10 feet long and 8 feet high shall also be added as a token of appreciation, which will be worthy of my lord's house.'

For reasons unexplained, Huygens did not wish to accept the gift, but Rembrandt was adamant. 'I cordially remain obliged to you to repay your lordship with service and friendship. Because I wish to do this, I am sending this accompanying canvas, against my lord's wishes, hoping that you will not take me amiss in this as it is the first token which I offer my lord.' He adds a postscript: 'My lord hang the piece in a strong light and so that one can stand at a distance from it, then it will show at its best.' The gift is 43    probably the painting of *The Blinding of Samson*, which was finished in 1636. In the very first letter written in that year, Rembrandt had said that 'I cannot refrain, as a token of my humble favour, from presenting my lord with something of my latest work, trusting that this will be accepted as favourably as possible.' Perhaps Rembrandt always had it in mind to present this picture to Huygens. It certainly matched the violence of expression of Rubens' head of *Medusa* which already hung in Huygens' house and was his favourite picture.

But no sooner were Frederick Henry's pictures finished than trouble arose over the price to be paid and the actual payment of the money. For the first two paintings Rembrandt received 1,200 guilders. But six years later he felt that the two last pictures 'will be considered of such quality that His Highness will now even pay me not less than a thousand guilders each. But should His Highness consider they are not worth this, he shall pay me less according to his own pleasure.' This request met with silence. In the meantime, Rembrandt had bought a house and the first payment was due on the day that he took possession. Time was drawing near, so he wrote again at the end of January: 'I would request you, my lord, that, whatever

41 *The Resurrection*, 1639

His Highness grants me for the two pieces, I may receive this money here as soon as possible, which would at the moment be particularly convenient to me.' One senses the perennial predicament of the artist, desperately in need of payment yet fearful of giving offence.

It was then that an admirer of Rembrandt's stepped in and tried to help. 'The tax collector, Uytenbogaert, paid me a visit when I was busy packing these two pieces. He wished to have a look at them first. He said that if it pleased His Highness he was prepared to make the payments from his office here [i.e. Amsterdam].' This Uytenbogaert was also called Jan, and was a distant relation of the Arminian preacher who had been Frederick Henry's tutor, portrayed by Rembrandt. He was the Receiver-General of state funds in Amsterdam and therefore in a position to help. He took up the matter of the delay in payment with Frederick Henry's Treasurer, and it may well have been in gratitude for his help that Rembrandt etched his portrait in this year. It is not in fact a straightforward portrait but has more of the character of an allegorical genre scene. The sitter is shown in sixteenth-century costume reminiscent of earlier representations of tax-collectors, and the print has for long been known as *The Goldweigher*. (He remained friendly with the artist; over ten years later his country house, which was situated outside Amsterdam, appears in the background of a landscape etching by Rembrandt.)

42

Rembrandt's price was ruthlessly cut down. 'If His Highness cannot in all decency be moved to a higher price, though they are obviously worth it, I shall be satisfied with 600 Carolus guilders each, provided that I am also credited for my outlay on the two ebony frames and the crate, which is 44 guilders in all. So I would kindly request of my lord that I may now receive my payments here in Amsterdam as soon as possible.' A little later to Huygens again: 'It is with hesitation that I come to trouble you with my letter . . . I pray you, my kind lord, that my warrant might now be prepared at once, so that I may now at least receive my well-earned 1,244 guilders.' Rembrandt need not have worried, for on 17 February Huygens had authorized the Treasurer to pay out the exact sum.

Rembrandt ends his last letter with the words 'With this I cordially take leave of my lord, and express that God may long [keep] your lordship in good health and bless you (Amen). Your lordship's humble and affectionate servant Rembrandt.' Throughout the correspondence the tone is respectful and formal. The artist never expands as one friend might to another. His farewell to Huygens was, so far as Rembrandt was concerned, only intended to mark the end of this particular affair, but for us with the advantage of hindsight it has a touching finality since so far as we know this letter is the last communication between the two men. In the next decade,

42 *Jan Uytenbogaert, the Receiver-General,* 1639

Rembrandt was asked to do two more paintings for Frederick Henry, but Huygens never intervened. A few years later, after the Stadholder's death, his widow made Huygens responsible for selecting artists to decorate the Oranjesaal in 'The House in the Woods' outside The Hague. Rembrandt was never considered, though Lievens amongst others was invited to contribute. Nevertheless Rembrandt's name was not entirely forgotten in the Huygens household, and in 1645 his son Christian, then sixteen, claimed with pride that he had copied the head of an old man by Rembrandt that 'can hardly be distinguished from the original'.

In spite of his taste for Flemish painting, it is disappointing that the one person to notice and understand Rembrandt's art and to forecast his greatness when the artist was only a young man of twenty-three should not so much turn against the artist as completely ignore him for the last thirty years of his life. Perhaps the more contemplative mood of *The Entombment*, heralding his new style, left Huygens unmoved. To us Huygens seems to have been a man whose genuine artistic sensibility and intuition were limited by the conventional taste of the time. But possibly the most curious aspect of their relationship is that the only picture by Rembrandt which we know Huygens possessed was pressed on him against his will.

The work produced for Frederick Henry and the gift to Huygens demonstrate the course of Rembrandt's art during the 1630s. Whereas Lastman appears as the main source of influence during the Leiden years, Rembrandt, without entirely forgetting his former master, seems to have turned much more to the example of Rubens after his move. Apart from the political wisdom of doing so, the Flemish master provided inspiration for a grander, more dramatic style which Rembrandt sought in the early Amsterdam years. Rubens' *Tribute Money* may, as has been suggested, have offered some hint for the composition of *The Anatomy Lesson of Professor Tulp*, and certainly he could give a lesson or two in the problems of foreshortening a figure. A more tangible link, already remarked, occurs in *The Descent from the Cross* in the following year, and in a more general way Rubens' oeuvre would have demonstrated the impact produced by a series of religious pictures and may indeed have prompted the idea of such a commission in the first place. But perhaps more important than any specific connections was Rubens' general example. There seems little doubt that Rembrandt studied both the latter's art and practice, although not surprisingly the end result tells us more about him.

In executing such works as *The Anatomy Lesson of Professor Tulp* and *The Descent from the Cross*, Rembrandt could have found a precedent for the smooth brushwork and plastic modelling, as well as the vivid, clearly identifiable expressions which were so much an essential ingredient in Rubens' religious painting. But where Rembrandt moved away from the latter was over the matter of realistic representation. Rubens believed in containing his artistic vocabulary within the classical convention. In the two versions of *The Descent from the Cross*, Rubens' Christ is a muscular, well-proportioned figure in the Italian tradition, whereas Rembrandt presents a sagging mass of inert flesh picked out from the penumbra by a strong light from above. In place of timeless balance, we become aware of

18

40

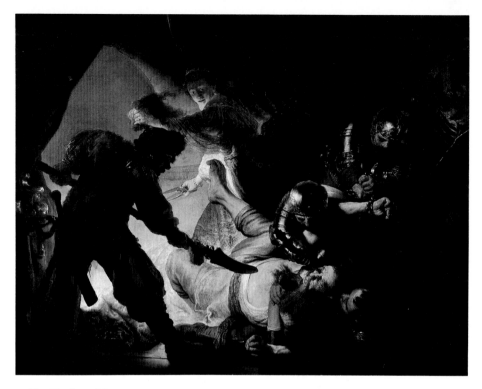

43 *The Blinding of Samson*, 1636

the suddenness of the moment. As with realism so with chiaroscuro; Rembrandt was prepared to go to extremes at this stage of his career.

The apogee of Rembrandt's Baroque style was reached in *The Blinding of Samson*, in which the climax of the highly disagreeable story is presented on life-size scale and with an unprecedented degree of realism. The artist's imagination operates on a theatrical level. The vast canvas is a maelstrom of violent contrasts – of movement, diagonal against diagonal, of chiaroscuro, *contre-jour* beside highlight, of colour, bright red juxtaposed with yellow, and of expression, searing physical pain alternating with refulgent triumph. The thickly loaded brush powerfully conveys the sumptuous effects of costume, shining armour, chains and various military accoutrements. Such intentional excess left little scope for further development.

This picture was one of three painted on the theme of Samson at this period and in its choice of subject matter reveals a characteristically Baroque preoccupation with an Old Testament hero whose life was so

65

44 ANON. *The Last Supper, after Leonardo da Vinci*, 16th century

45 *The Last Supper, after Leonardo da Vinci, c.* 1635

46 *Samson's Wedding Feast*, 1638

redolent with high drama and sensuality. (Concurrently when treating the life of Christ, Rembrandt opted for elaborate crowd-scenes, such as *The Preaching of St John the Baptist*, in which display rather than quiet mystery provided the *donnée*.) Returning to the theme of Samson in 1638, Rembrandt maintained the sense of drama in *Samson's Wedding Feast*, here enhanced by richness of colour, although he introduced more variety and subtlety into his composition. The manner in which Delilah, seated before a hanging carpet, presides over her guests deployed on either side of her in a variety of postures, a placid unperturbed figure floating above a sea of animation, recalls the free copies Rembrandt made after an engraving of Leonardo's *Last Supper*. Although more complex in its counterpoint of movement, and very different in detail, *Samson's Wedding Feast* is unequivocally recognizable as a Baroque heir to a major monument of the High Renaissance.

But Rembrandt was equally concerned with content, and a few years after it was painted, *Samson's Wedding Feast* was referred to in a speech delivered in Leiden as an excellent example of a work by an artist who from knowledge and attention had produced an accurate re-creation of the story, full of historical detail. 'The Ancients used little beds to lie on, and they did not sit at Table as we do now, but reclined on their elbows.' Samson, immediately recognizable in his unshorn state, 'is busy propounding his Riddle . . . [with] a common but very natural gesture'. And the speaker concluded his oration: 'He made a distinction so that we could well distinguish it from our own wedding feasts. Behold this fruit of his own natural expression derived from history well read and understood by high and far [reaching] reflection.'

In the course of his correspondence with Huygens, Rembrandt wrote at the beginning of 1639 that he was at last proposing to deliver *The Entombment* and *The Resurrection*, in which 'the greatest and most natural movement (or most innate emotion) has been expressed'. Whether the artist meant 'movement' or 'emotion' remains a subject of philological debate, although in this instance both meanings are relevant, since the first is appropriate to the frenzy of light and action in *The Resurrection* whereas the second would fit the intensity of feeling which can be read in the expressions and actions of those surrounding the figure of the dead Christ. In their different ways the two pictures follow the Baroque convention established at the beginning of the series. But as he was finishing them, he must have been aware that his art was moving in a different direction, and at least in much of their execution they point to the future.

The same characteristics can be perceived in his drawings and etchings of the period. After moving to Amsterdam, Rembrandt soon developed drawing as a means of expression in its own right and produced a series of Biblical subjects which are concerned more with the interpretation of the subject than as an exercise in style. This preoccupation with content could very well be expressed in a medium in which economy of line could be an essential feature. In the drawing of *Calvary* he forcefully conveys emotion through the character of the pen lines supported by the addition of wash. The dead Christ on the cross, a catalyst in the scene around Him, is relatively neatly drawn and modelled. His calm acceptance of fate is thrown into relief by the intensely distraught reactions of His immediate companions, whose figures are suggested more than defined by what appears as a frenzy of lines heightened by bold strokes of wash. Through the direction of his pen lines enhanced by a lively pattern of shadow, Rembrandt creates a feeling of circular movement in the crowd beneath the figure on the cross rising above in solitary state.

On a large scale etching proved, to begin with, a less individual medium. But on a small scale he could work in much the same way as in a drawing, and during these years he developed a style which paralleled rather than

47 *Calvary, c.* 1635

48 *The Annunciation to the Shepherds*, 1634

imitated what he was producing with his pen. But his real battle with the medium was fought in a series of large plates etched during the decade in which he gradually succeeded in using the innate character of the etched line. At first he sought the qualities of a painting, and it was consistent with his purpose that he should set out to reproduce one of his works for the Stadholder, *The Descent from the Cross*. (And in executing this sizeable task, almost certainly carried out without assistance, he was forced through

49 *The Death of the Virgin*, 1639

some technical failure in the biting to abandon the first plate and start all
48  over again.) In *The Annunciation to the Shepherds* the style is still painterly in
the highly wrought nocturnal landscape seen by moonlight above which
the heavens literally open in a blaze of light to reveal the Angel as well as a
host of younger angels. But whereas the prevailing dark areas stretch the
technical possibilities to the utmost, more intrinsically etched work
describes the shepherds and their animals instilled with terror.

49      In *The Death of the Virgin* of 1639, Rembrandt succeeded by employing a
looser more varied stroke to combine the miraculous appearance of the
angels above, the formal ritual of a Christian death and the very human
event of a dying person surrounded by sorrowing companions. His new
command of technique enabled him to join spiritual and earthly in a
Baroque extravagance tempered by a new intimacy of feeling.

   Although Rembrandt, in whichever medium he was working, gave a
dramatic overlay of chiaroscuro and action to his finished works of the
1630s, his art was founded on an accurate observation of the world around
him. *St John the Baptist preaching*, a grisaille painted in the middle of the

50 *The Preaching of St John the Baptist* (detail), *c.* 1636

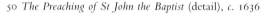

51 *Woman with a Child frightened by a Dog, c. 1635*

decade possibly in preparation for an etching, possesses with its profusion of incident the character of other pictures of the time. But if the veil of richly varied shadow is removed, a remarkable range of studies of the impoverished, sick, old and very young will be revealed. It is no coincidence that during this decade Rembrandt was most active as an observer of everyday life. Although there are a number of etchings, he mostly used drawing for this study, largely using the quill pen with its varied repertory of loops and curves. Such studies done without ulterior purpose provided him with a basic artistic vocabulary which could be adapted to the work in hand. Numerous studies of women and children, such as that of a mother, basket over her arm, who reassures her child fearful at the approach of a friendly dog, provided him with the kind of knowledge necessary for the vignettes of domestic life which occur in the grisaille.

The artist's observation of the daily scene had already begun in Leiden, and there are a number of drawings and etchings of beggars, those nomadic victims of the political upheavals throughout the Continent. In one etching

53 *Jew praying, c.* 1634

52 *Beggar warming his Hands, c.* 1630

54 *Two Butchers at Work, c.* 1635

55 *The Pancake Woman*, 1635

an elderly beggar, his worldly possessions in a basket, sits warming his hands over a chafing dish. Although inspired by Callot both in subject and technique, Rembrandt's treatment avoids the political overtones of the French artist and concentrates on representing them as human beings, albeit as the more unhappy members of the rich fabric of seventeenth-century society. In Amsterdam his acute observation grew in response to the varied scene to be found in such a cosmopolitan city. He developed a particular interest in the Jews, those authentic descendants of the Old Testament. Whereas he received commissions from the more prosperous Sephardim the impoverished Ashkenazim provided endless models of grizzled old age and wisdom gained from a silent acceptance of fate. In one small but penetrating study a youngish Jew kneels devoutly with hands 53 clasped in prayer – his earnest submissive expression caught with a few rapid lines of the quill pen.

56 *A Negro Commander and Kettle-Drummer on Horseback,* c. 1638

57 *Elephant,* c. 1637

58 *A Scene from Vondel's 'Gijsbrecht van Amstel', c.* 1638

59 *Swimmers*, 1651

Rembrandt's graphic works of these years indicate that the artist was constantly on the lookout for all manner of daily occurrence as he wandered through the streets. In one study he observes two butchers at work; one squatting on his haunches cleaving a carcass, while the other, knife held in his mouth, struggles to move another carcass. The etching of *The Pancake Woman* captures the essence of a scene to be discovered at many a street corner – the concentration of the chef surrounded by her hungry admiring audience, while at her feet a child saves its pancake from an importunate dog. Performances by travelling circuses were a regular occurrence in Amsterdam and they probably provided the models for the small group of animal studies, such as the drawing of an elephant, with its masterly use of black chalk to describe the wrinkled skin. The procession in The Hague in 1638, already mentioned, prompted, it would seem, the studies of exotic mounted musicians, such as the *Negro Commander and Kettle-Drummer on Horseback*, executed in an unusually rich mixture of pen,

54

55

57

56

60 *A Woman on the Gallows*, 1664

chalk and colour. The same year witnessed the inauguration of Jacob van Campen's splendid new theatre built in the classical style, which replaced the old wooden building used by the Dutch Academy. Given the character of Rembrandt's art at this time, he probably found much to stir his imagination in the theatre. One may suppose that the *mise-en-scène* of some of his more elaborate compositions of this time reflects the theatrical spectacle at least in the community of interest if not actual derivation. In addition there are a number of drawings, which can be identified as studies

58  of actors, such as the pen and wash portrayal of a bishop who may represent the central character in Vondel's play *Gijsbrecht van Amstel*, which opened the new theatre.

In later years Rembrandt devoted less time to the outdoor scene. Apart from his new preoccupations, his portfolios of drawings, representing his working capital, already contained an encyclopaedia of everyday life. But his interest did not entirely disappear, and every now and then a particular incident caught his attention. In one of his most atmospheric etchings, three

59  naked young men take a dip in the river bordered by trees. And five years before Rembrandt's death, a Danish girl was condemned to the gallows for

60  murder, and he made two drawings of her, one from the front and one from the side, as she hung limp with her axe beside her.

For all its apparent fidelity to nature, Dutch art contained a moralizing side, replete with allegory and emblem. For the most part Rembrandt was

61 *Death appearing to a Wedded Couple*, 1639

62 *The Unity of the Country*, 1641

not in sympathy with such an approach. With his habitual width of interest he has left several works which clearly bear more meaning than is apparent at first glance, but in several cases their meaning eludes us today. Some form of personal allegory seems to have been intended in the small etching of *Death appearing to a Wedded Couple*. Political allegory was clearly the basis of the grisaille known from the artist's inventory as *The Unity of the Country* (more usually translated as *The Concord of State*). Apart from references to religion, justice, political order and military power, the founding principles of the Republic, the picture is centred around the figure of the recumbent lion, a symbol of the Netherlands, placed before coats of arms of the three main cities of the state of Holland – Amsterdam, Leiden and Haarlem. The five of the Seven United Provinces governed by Frederick Henry are alluded to by the five arrows beneath the lion's paw. The picture, whose purpose remains unknown, can be interpreted as an allegory of the current political struggle between the State of Holland and the Stadholder over the latter's costly military campaigns.

## CHAPTER THREE

## A change of direction

In 1639, the year that Rembrandt took his leave of Huygens, an important artistic event took place in Amsterdam, when 'the whole cargo', as Rembrandt called it, of Lucas van Uffelen came up for auction. The seller, who had originally come from Antwerp, had spent a number of years in Venice, active as a banker, shipper and collector of works of art before he settled in Holland. Rembrandt attended the sale and even though he did not 63 buy anything consoled himself by making a free copy of one of the pictures, either at the time or, more likely in view of the variations, from memory in the studio after the sale. Beside his sketch he wrote: 'The Count Balthasar Castiglione by Raphael, sold for 3,500 guilders'. The successful bidder was Alphonso Lopez. The underbidder was none other than Joachim von Sandrart, the German painter and writer on art.

Alphonso Lopez was a rich Spanish Jew who lived in a large house on the Singel in Amsterdam. He was a diamond dealer as well as a collector, art dealer, and working as agent for Richelieu on behalf of the French crown, for whom he bought anything from ammunition to works of art. Lopez 69 already owned Titian's so-called *Portrait of Ariosto*, as well as Rembrandt's 12 *Balaam and the Ass* painted as long before as 1626. We do not know when he bought it from the artist but in 1641 the French artist Claude Vignon wrote to a French print publisher and art dealer: 'In Amsterdam also give my regards to Mynheer Rembrandt and bring back something of his. Tell him simply that yesterday I appraised his painting of the prophet Balaam which Monsieur Lopez bought from him.'

Lopez and Rembrandt must have known one another, since Lopez's Titian made a profound effect on Rembrandt at this time. In the self-portrait etching of 1639 and in the repetition, with a few alterations, on 70 canvas the following year, Rembrandt has depicted himself in a similar pose with the arm resting on a ledge, while the arrangement and treatment of his sleeve show an obvious debt to the Venetian picture. At the same time Rembrandt transformed his version into his own idiom by introducing a more varied pattern of chiaroscuro especially in the background, as well as employing a different and much more restricted colour scheme. He also included such Baroque touches as the arrangement

63 *Copy after Raphael's 'Portrait of Baldassare Castiglione', 1639*

of the sleeve so that it falls over the parapet into the spectator's world. The conscious allusion to Titian's portrait, which must have been as obvious to people in Amsterdam at the time as Brahms' echo of Beethoven in his first symphony two centuries later, may signify more than an adaptation of the outward form of a major High Renaissance work. At the period the Titian was thought to represent the distinguished Ferrarese poet Ludovico Ariosto and it has been proposed that not only was Rembrandt consciously rivalling the achievement of a famous painter of the past, but in associating himself with Ariosto he was proclaiming a parity between the art of painting and literature. The battle for the status and dignity of the artist was still not entirely won, and some of the tradition of the artist as craftsman lingered on in the rules and practices of the guilds of St Luke.

In this self-portrait Rembrandt presents himself as a serious almost solemn figure with a far more dignified and flattering image than is to be seen in the portrait by his pupil, Govaert Flinck, painted in the previous

64 Govaert Flinck *Portrait of Rembrandt* (detail), 1639

year. It possesses more than a touch of elegance and *hauteur*, and the piercing gaze implies equality with whomever the spectator might be. Flinck portrayed the artist, whereas Rembrandt depicts the gentleman. But his position was now established and he had become a much-praised artist, both by his fellow-countrymen and foreigners. An English visitor to Amsterdam in 1640, who had no pretensions to knowledge of art, writes of the flourishing state of painting in Holland, but mentions only one artist by name and that is Rembrandt. Though a grave expression was becoming to the fashionable painter of the day, it signified something far deeper in Rembrandt's case. A profound metamorphosis was taking place in his art. He was slowly turning away from all that his painting stood for in the 1630s to a new more personal style. It took a number of years to achieve, but already the alchemy of searching self-analysis was taking effect. As he followed his own vision unheedingly, as any artist of integrity or greatness must do, so he deliberately moved out of the orbit of fashionable taste and merited its indifference, a reaction which one suspects was much encouraged by his growing intransigence and unwillingness to please.

The more thoughtful mood could also be the effect of family responsibilities. By the time he wrote his first letter to Huygens in 1636 he and Saskia had left her cousin's house in the Breestraat and were living in the Nieuwe Doelenstraat. By the end of the following year they had moved again to the island of Vlooienburgh; Rembrandt wrote to Huygens 65 that 'I live on the Binnen Amstel. The house is called the sugar refinery.' At that time this building offered spectacular views of the river and the quays, with a vista of the countryside beyond the Blauwbrug (a view seen in a later drawing, p. 107). But once again it was a temporary residence, and on 3 January 1639 he bought his well-known house in the Breestraat and 67 moved in on 1 May. The purchase of this property was to be a turning-point in his financial fortunes, although at the time it did not seem an unreasonable expense in view of his income and success which promised further rewards. The house was acquired jointly from the original owner's son and son-in-law, Peter Belten jr and Christoffel Thijsz, both of whom were wealthy merchants. Belten was also yet another partner in Van Ulenborch's art dealing firm. The contract specified that within a year Rembrandt would repay in three instalments one-quarter of the purchase price of 13,000 guilders, and that the remaining three-quarters would be repaid when and as Rembrandt pleased within five or six years, but the unpaid sum would attract interest at the rate of 5%. The cause of much of Rembrandt's future trouble was that he was never able to keep to these terms.

No doubt Rembrandt was particularly happy to move back to the street where he had spent his first years. His new house was situated next door to Van Ulenborch's, so their social intercourse could have known no bounds. But as well as Van Ulenborch there were a number of other friends and patrons in the street. The district had always had aristocratic inhabitants and in the seventeenth century was gradually taken over by wealthy, highly cultured Portuguese Jewish families, among whom was Rembrandt's friend Menasseh ben Israel. By the end of the century the name of the street had been changed from the St Anthoniesbreestraat to the

65 Balthasar van Berckenrode *Map of Amsterdam* (detail), 1625

66 Zeeman *St Anthoniespoort, Amsterdam,* 1636

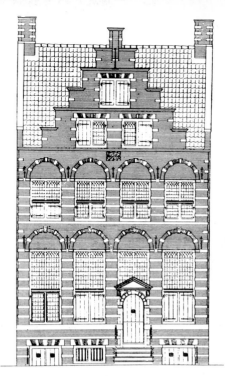

67 The front of Rembrandt's house in the St Anthoniesbreestraat, Amsterdam

68 Rembrandt's house in the Breestraat as it must have looked

Joden(Jews)breestraat. And in the way that fashion moves from one district to another so this quarter, though still remaining predominantly Jewish, has taken on an aspect of picturesque poverty. The flea market which is now held round the corner would have been unthinkable in the seventeenth century. At the end of the street was the Anthoniespoort (seen in an etching by Zeeman), one of the main exits from the city, and beyond lay the open country of the Diemerdyke, leading to small towns such as Diemen and Muiden.

Today the house, which had been built in 1607, serves as a poor reminder of its original occupant. Its former atmosphere is not suggested by the modern panelling and the lack of contemporary furniture. More important are the alterations which have been made to the exterior. Instead of the cornice with a Classical pediment which we see today, there was originally a stepped gable in the manner of the earlier seventeenth-century houses. This change, probably carried out a few years before Rembrandt's death, would hardly have pleased him if he could ever bring himself to walk along the street where so much of his life had taken place.

69 Titian
*Portrait of a Man, c.* 1512

Financial difficulties were not his sole domestic worry. Two of their children had already died and the third one born that year was to live an even shorter time. Saskia must have despaired of giving birth to a child that would live. The numerous drawings of her lying in bed may well signify 71 frequent illnesses. One of the most complete of these, a genre picture in itself, shows Saskia lying in bed with hands clasped before her and her features displaying weakness if not actual pain. At the foot of the bed on a stool by the fireplace sits a nurse, one of those large round-faced comforting bodies who whiles away her time knitting. At the head of the bed there is an empty chair, clearly the master's. The fireplace with caryatids supporting the mantelpiece on the extreme left identifies the scene as taking place in their new house. The drawing was probably made shortly after they had moved in. Cornelia II was born in July and a few

70 *Self-portrait*, 1640

weeks later was dead. It is not too far-fetched to identify Saskia's unhappy look with this painful event.

One of Saskia's constant companions during these years was her sister, Titia, who was married to François Coopal, Commissioner in Middelburg, brother of Frederick Henry's secret agent. Titia was clearly her favourite sister. She was witness *in absentia* at the baptism of Saskia's first two children and their fourth child Titus was named after his aunt. She obviously spent much time in the Rembrandt household, and on one of these occasions Rembrandt drew her portrait. It is a charmingly informal study, the kind of drawing he might have made after dinner as the family sat talking. Titia, head bent forward, is engrossed in her sewing, her pince-nez propped on the end of her nose. Clearly the drawing gave pleasure, for the artist wrote her name and the date underneath.

An unintended presentiment of what was to come occurs in the curiously personal allegory of *Death appearing to a Wedded Couple from an Open Grave*. The husband leads his wife towards the skeleton, who holds up an hourglass to show that her time has come. The husband is about to take farewell of his wife as she descends the steps to the grave. She is

71 *Saskia's Bedroom, c.* 1639

72 *Titia van Ulenborch*

73 *Saskia Ill, c.* 1642

elegantly dressed, in a decorative hat, and she holds a flower with all the solemnity of an acolyte bearing a candle. Too soon to be relevant to the artist's own life, it probably refers to the death of the wife of a friend or pupil.

Death certainly struck at Rembrandt's and Saskia's families. In the same year as the death of their second daughter Rembrandt's mother died. We do not know how much mother and son saw of one another in later years. Probably not very much since there are no records of any visits to Leiden, and the mother was not named as a witness at the baptism of either her second or third granddaughters, both of whom were named after her. The following year Titia died. But in September of that year there was one great consolation, the birth of Titus, their only child to escape the net of infant mortality.

Perhaps the birth of Titus was responsible for Saskia's final illness. An etching which must have been made about this time shows her in an advanced stage of sickness. The plump cheeks of her earlier years are gone, her face is thin, her cheeks hollow, and her expression haggard. On 14 June 1642 she died, eight years almost to the very day after they were married in Friesland. She was buried five days later in the Oude Kerk.

Saskia made her will a few days before her death. By common law half of their joint estate, which amounted to more than 40,000 guilders, belonged to Rembrandt, although there is no indication how much of this derived from Saskia's inheritance and how much from Rembrandt's earnings. Saskia left her half to Titus, allowing Rembrandt the *usufruct* until Titus either came of age or married, but the former would lose these benefits should he remarry. Other clauses in the will testify to Saskia's complete confidence in Rembrandt, which must surely reflect the harmony of their marriage. He was to remain the sole guardian of Titus. He was exempted from accounting for the administration of the estate and from preparing any inventory of possessions as she was certain that he would carry out her wishes. The latter exemption proved shortsighted and a list had to be hastily prepared five years later. And her final decree was that the Chamber of Orphans, the usual guardians of such estates, was specifically denied any involvement. Like so many wills made with the best intentions it was the cause of much hardship to the very person it was meant to favour.

Such was the pressure of domestic affairs during the three years before Saskia's death that Rembrandt would have had good cause to neglect his art. But both the quantity and quality of the work he produced at this time show that this is far from what happened. It was during this time that he reached a turning-point in his career as an artist, and in the very year of Saskia's death painted his largest and most ambitious work.

A few doors away from the house that Rembrandt and Saskia inhabited in the Nieuwe Doelenstraat stood the Kloveniersdoelen, which housed the militia company of *arquebusiers* or musketeers. The front of the building 28 can be seen in the drawing, half-way down on the right, set back from the road. The back of the house, which bordered the River Amstel, known at 74 this point as the Binnen Amstel, appears in a contemporary engraving. The tower on the right in the engraving is one of the old fortifications of the city, known as Zwijgt-Utrecht (Be silent Utrecht), which was the subject 97 of a later drawing by Rembrandt. To the immediate left is the handsome

74 JACOB VAN MEURS
The Kloveniersdoelen, Amsterdam

75 ANON. The House of
Captain F. Banning Cocq

new wing of the Doelen only completed in 1636, which contained one of the most spacious interiors in the city.

Although retaining some of their guard duties the militia companies had in the years of relative peace become increasingly ceremonial in function. Nevertheless they retained their image as the defenders of the city and its privileges which they had done so much to achieve during the establishment of the republic. At the time the company of *arquebusiers* was under the command of Captain Frans Banning Cocq, a wealthy and ambitious man without occupation, who lived in an unusually grand house on the Singel, built by Hendrick de Keyser at the beginning of the century. By an advantageous marriage he acquired wealth, property and titles, and he rapidly established himself as a member of the city hierarchy, which eventually led to a term as burgomaster. His rise in the militia was no less speedy and his assumption of the command of the company took place shortly after the completion of the new wing of the Doelen, which between 1639 and 1645 was decorated with eight militia groups. As well as to Rembrandt, commissions were given to his former pupils, Backer and Flinck, to the fashionable portrait painter Bartholomeus van der Helst and to the German Joachim von Sandrart. Until their removal in the eighteenth century, these eight canvasses provided the most impressive image of the status of the militia, in which most of the rich and powerful of the city were represented. This grand scheme of decoration was also to prove the swansong of the militia, who within a decade had declined as a force in city affairs.

The choice of Rembrandt among others was a clear acknowledgment of his continuing standing as an artist in Amsterdam. This major commission almost certainly given by December 1640 occupied him until at least the middle of 1642. The picture, which has acquired the popular and incorrect title of *The Night Watch*, shows, in the words of the commanding officer,

76 BARTHOLOMEUS VAN DER HELST *The Company of Captain Roelof Bicker*, 1639

77 'The Night Watch', 1642

'the young Heer van Purmerandt [Banning Cocq] as captain, ordering his lieutenant, the Heer van Vlaerdingen [Willem van Ruytenburch], to march the company out', during, we may add, daylight. Both the moment it showed – this was no artificially posed group but a call to arms with real-life extras such as dogs and children – and the subordination of portraiture to the whole composition were revolutionary. We know each sitter paid a contribution consistent with his prominence in the picture, and we can be sure that this kind of body would have been no less conservative than their counterpart today. In fact no grumbles from the sitters have reached our ears. On the contrary, Banning Cocq had a watercolour copy made for his album, and two of his men testified on the artist's behalf over fifteen years later about the fee paid. Neither is the action of a dissatisfied client.

96

Several contemporary critics attest to the picture's importance in Rembrandt's oeuvre. Baldinucci twice says it was famous on the basis of what Keil told him. Rembrandt's pupil Samuel van Hoogstraten provides a more circumstantial assessment of its virtues and failings. Although believing that 'it is not enough for a painter to place his figures next to each other in a row, as can be found here in Holland all too often in the civic-guard halls', he criticized Rembrandt for an excess of originality in making the picture 'too much according to his own wishes' rather than concentrating on the individual portraits. Nevertheless Rembrandt's picture 'will survive all its competitors because it is so painter-like in thought, so ingenious in the varied placement of figures, and so powerful that in comparison, according to some, all the other pieces there (i.e., in the Doelen) look like packs of playing cards.' In other words Rembrandt stole the show, as a comparison with the 'pack of playing cards' produced by Van der Helst all too clearly demonstrates.

Rembrandt transformed the traditional arrangement of a group of portraits, bearing allusions to the sitters' various duties in the company, into a scene replete with action illustrating the role of each participant. Apart from the seemingly naturalistic portrayal of the militia group itself, Rembrandt has introduced a number of symbolic extras such as the girl with the Kloveniers' emblem of claws suspended at her waist, the drummer whose presence refers to festive occasions and the varying positions in which the muskets are held, taken from arms manuals of the period. The massive archway in the background acts as a symbol of the city gate to be defended, at the same time as it articulates the composition before it. It is a work of rich Baroque complexity in which realism and symbolism are skilfully combined in a masterly integration of movement, light and colour, harmonized by an intricate pattern of chiaroscuro. In these respects it represents the apogee in Rembrandt's painting.

About the time Rembrandt moved into his new house in the Breestraat, he began to look at the city around him, as well as the country and small villages in the vicinity of Amsterdam. Landscape was not an entirely new departure for him. He had already done a few paintings and some drawings. But quite apart from being few in number, they lacked a sense of locality. To judge by these works Rembrandt might have lived almost anywhere in Holland. It was as if he suddenly woke up to the beauty and character of his surroundings, and for approximately the next fifteen years he threw himself into a passionate study, in drawing and etching with an occasional painting, of not just impersonalized landscape but of a definite locality. He analysed the city and its environs in a way that has been equalled in intensity only by Cézanne in Aix-en-Provence. To follow him in his walks even today, when so much has been destroyed or built over, is one of the pleasures of Rembrandt 'at home'.

What was the reason for this sudden awakening of interest? One can guess that a small factor may have been the effect of ownership of property. Rembrandt must have walked around Amsterdam hundreds of times and probably often along the Breestraat through the Anthoniespoort and out on to the Diemerdyke where he was surrounded by open country. But hitherto he never felt a desire to record the landscape and the buildings he saw. Perhaps in the way that ownership of a house inspires a direct interest in one's neighbourhood, so moving back to the Breestraat, but into a house of his own, may have stimulated in Rembrandt a desire to record the background of the human scene that he studied so exhaustively in his drawings of the previous decade.

The anxieties of the domestic scene may also have contributed. Rembrandt perhaps found in those wide open windy views around Amsterdam a relaxation from the sickbed and a preparation for what fate had in store for him. Again, the loneliness of his life for several years after Saskia's death may have been relieved by such outside activities. A passionate study of landscape possibly offered a welcome escapist world removed from the scene of his unhappiness.

But if personal reasons for this new taste played their part, we can be sure their contribution was only a small one. Artistic interests were far more important. The new searching, introspective mood was already seen in the self-portrait of 1640. To achieve this Rembrandt developed a much simpler style, eschewing theatrical gesture, and concentrating far more on describing the inner emotion recalled in tranquillity. Landscape provided an admirable means of reaching the desired goal. The myriad forms of nature must of necessity be simplified by the landscape artist. Rembrandt continued the process until his landscape was described by no more than a few strokes. By that time he had exhausted the subject and had achieved his purpose.

An interest in landscape developed in Rembrandt's work in the late 1630s, when apart from some drawings he produced a small group of paintings mainly of imaginary mountainous scenery. These offered fantasies in the spirit of Hercules Seghers, whose work Rembrandt collected and admired, and who can be recognized as the primary source of inspiration in this early phase of landscape. Occasionally the subject was
78   more realistic, as in the *Landscape with a Stone Bridge*, which was based on the scenery of a tributary of the Amstel near Ouderkerk, a locality which was shortly to provide such a rich seam of motifs. Nevertheless the realities of the view are depicted in an unusual colour scheme and hidden beneath

78 *Landscape with a Stone Bridge, c.* 1638

dramatically contrasting effects of sunlight and stormclouds, found in other landscapes of the period, and match the chiaroscuro of other contemporary work. Thereafter in the few landscapes he painted, Rembrandt kept to the imaginary, although his one very small example of a *Winter Landscape*, painted in 1646, offers such a brilliant gem-like image 79 of ice and clear cold light that we are almost persuaded that it must have been based on an actual view on a particular day. Significantly it provides human interest hardly less important than the landscape itself.

The exploration of landscape was primarily carried out in prints and drawings over the course of about thirteen years stretching from 1640 to 1653. The etchings were primarily made in two bursts of activity, from 1640 to 1645 and again from 1650 to 1653, whereas he was probably making drawings over the whole of the period. In simplifying and arranging the forms of the landscape Rembrandt started by placing the centre of interest in the foreground and creating a sense of distance from this point. In later works he removed his motif, frequently a farmhouse or building set among trees, that ubiquitous feature of the Dutch countryside, some way back in his composition. He presented a more measured and monumental assessment of his theme by establishing space in the foreground and providing atmospheric vistas to the sides. Instead of a preoccupation with surface pattern he sought the effects of distance and air.

For drawing Rembrandt started by using both chalk and the quill pen. The former was a particularly suitable medium for the sketchbooks he used in the early years. Like his study of humanity he began with the raw material outside his house. But he soon abandoned chalk for pen and at the same time frequently changed from the quill, with its excellent descriptive line, to the soft broad stroke of the reed pen, which so admirably summarized the extent and scale of the landscape. These later works convey the very essence of space, light and atmosphere, the effects of which were enhanced by freely applied areas of translucent washes, only added, we may be sure, as the result of deliberate calculation. Unlike many of his contemporaries, Rembrandt never used watercolour and confined himself to either black or brown ink, very occasionally employing a combination of both. Sometimes in his late drawings the sheet of paper was prepared

79 *Winter Landscape*, 1646

80 *The Clump of Trees*, 1652

with a pale coloured wash, which produced a unifying tone mellower than the stark white of the actual paper.

In his landscape prints, Rembrandt began by using the etched line in much the same way as he did the quill pen, although being finer he required more lines for detail or emphasis, as can be seen in the early *View of Amsterdam*. The change to the reed pen for drawing was paralleled in his prints by the introduction of drypoint, a process of drawing directly into the copper plate. The furrows thrown up by the needle were retained to print rich velvet textures, which by skilful manipulation could convey a similar effect to that of the reed pen or an area of wash. This technique, usually employed in a combination with etching, as for example in the *Goldweigher's Field*, was occasionally used by itself to memorable effect as in *The Clump of Trees*. To obtain a similar quality to the drawings prepared with washes, Rembrandt printed on a wide variety of different papers. Above all he chose oriental papers of varying thicknesses, which apart

82 *View of Amsterdam, c.* 1640

from their yellowish colour, printed the accents of drypoint as a soft blur, and enhanced the portrayal of landscape forms suffused in atmosphere. In both his landscape prints and drawings all the technical resources were brilliantly harnessed to realize the pictorial purpose, and examples of his growing mastery are found in all aspects of his later works.

The practice of landscape invokes the question of whether the artist only worked in his studio or whether he painted, etched or drew before the motif, as was beginning to be done in the seventeenth century. Although it cannot be doubted that all the known pictures by Rembrandt were executed in the studio, there are tantalizing references in his inventory of 1656 to 'one landscape' and 'some houses', both described as 'painted from nature'. In the case of drawing it is likely that he followed both practices, either working exclusively in or out of doors depending on the work in hand, or sometimes starting before the subject and continuing in the studio, especially when he added elaborate washes. Etching is a far less tractable medium for outside work and the most we can probably envisage is that occasionally he may have drawn the outlines on the grounded plate before

103

83 *The Bulwark on the West of Amsterdam, c.* 1641

his motif. But work in drypoint could more easily be managed and it may be that the first state of *The Clump of Trees*, that roughly gouged image of bursting foliage, represents work before the subject, which was then completed in the studio in its second stage. But wherever Rembrandt worked, it can be clearly established that he took much of his subject matter from the countryside around Amsterdam.

84 *View over the River Y from the Diemerdyke, c.* 1650

Within an hour Rembrandt could reach on foot almost any site he drew, 81 and it is therefore impossible to say when he devoted his energies to one particular motif. Style only acts as a broad guide. Variety of purpose and lack of all but a few fixed points make it nearly impossible to say with any degree of conviction in what year an actual landscape drawing was done.

At first Rembrandt was more interested in landscape outside the city. One of his earliest views is the etching of Amsterdam. To get this view 82 Rembrandt left the Anthoniespoort and walked in a north-easterly direction until he reached the bastion 'de Rijsenhoofd', which was the outermost bulwark of Amsterdam. Once outside this point he would have reached the place from where he would have gained the view we see reversed in the etching. We see from left to right the Haringpakkerstoren, the Oude Kerk, Montelbaarnstoren, which Rembrandt was to draw on later, the warehouses of the East and West India Companies, the windmill on the Rijzenhoofd, which he had passed on his way, and finally the Zuiderkerk.

On another occasion Rembrandt made a walk to the other side of 83 Amsterdam and drew the Blauwhoofd. This consisted of a windmill and two cottages which can be seen on the map on the upper left. It was the first bulwark on the west side of Amsterdam and was situated at a point where the Prinsengracht now runs out into the River Y. In those days it commanded wonderful views. On one side there was the harbour with its forest of masts, and immediately near by shipbuilding yards. On the other it looked over the River Y with its constant shipping, and beyond to the open flat country to the north.

85 *View of Diemen, c.* 1650

This open landscape clearly attracted Rembrandt, because at another time, instead of going north-east immediately outside the Anthoniespoort, he continued along the Diemerdyke towards Diemen. At the end of the 84 dyke he reached the River Y, from where he made two drawings of the river to the north. (This view occurs as the background of another drawing to be mentioned later.) In the distance across the river can be seen the village of Spaarndam. Rembrandt wonderfully suggests the width of the river with its translucent quality set against the opacity and solidity of the river banks.

Quite often Rembrandt continued his walk past the Diemerdyke. After the road reaches the river, it turns abruptly south until it reaches Diemen. The church's square tower, surmounted by a spire, is easily recognizable. The village from every angle became one of the artist's favourite subjects. Here we see it from the north approaching along the road from Amsterdam. It is high summer. The hay barn is full. A milkman carries his churns along the road. Oxen plough the field. It is one of Rembrandt's most finished landscape drawings. Another walk which Rembrandt did frequently throughout his 'landscape years' was along the banks of the River Amstel to the village of Ouderkerk, the subject of an earlier painting. Fortunately this can still be done today, either on foot, or better, by boat,

86 *View of the River Amstel from the Blauwbrug, Amsterdam, c.* 1650

though the rapid growth of frankly ugly buildings this side of Amsterdam threatens to close in on one of the preserves for those who wish to recapture the atmosphere of former centuries.

One can start one's walk at the Blauwbrug, the bridge across the Amstel which in those days marked the south-eastern perimeter of the city. This was Rembrandt's starting-point, and he has left us three drawings of this view. The present study was taken from the middle of the bridge. The river stretches away towards Ouderkerk. Rembrandt suggests the width of the water by the horizontal lines of the mooring quays which reach out into midstream. On the left six boats are tied up, while in the middle of the river a rowing-boat moves towards us.

Yielding to the immediate temptation to follow where one's gaze is led in the drawing, one soon reaches a point where a canal known as the Ringvaart runs into the Amstel from the north side. A windmill and several houses used to stand on the little tongue of land formed by the canal and river, and were known as the Omval. Rembrandt drew this motif more than once at quite different times of his career. He must have walked past it very often. In the etching of 1645, the Omval is seen (in reverse) from the other side of the river. The mouth of the canal can be made out between the two windmills. It is a lively scene. There are sailing-boats and rowing-boats 87

87 *The Omval*, 1645

88 *The Bend in the River Amstel
with the House of Kostverloren
in the Trees, c.* 1650

on the far shore, while a stately barge covered with a canopy, perhaps carrying a family on a Sunday afternoon outing, proceeds up the river. On our side of the river a man stands and gazes, while, hidden in the foliage on the left, a young man crowns his beloved with a garland.

Beyond the river twists and bends, so that walking along the bank one has constantly changing views. About a mile farther up the river one used to reach a house set among the trees on the river bank, known as Kostverloren. This place more than any other was Rembrandt's chosen motif for drawing on the Amstel. The house had been burnt around the middle of the century and was in ruins, as one of his drawings shows. (The approximate place is marked today by the house called Amstelrust.) Rembrandt explored every aspect of this particular site at all seasons of the year. The present drawing is one of the most extensive views of this wide curve of the river, with its rich profusion of trees on the bank hiding the buildings. On the left the tower of Kostverloren can be made out against the skyline. Here Rembrandt gives us a study of the light on the water and trees. On other occasions it is the sculptural form which impresses.

On the back of another drawing made near this spot, his fellow artist, Philips Koninck, has written with all the certainty of an eye-witness: 'This drawing shows the bank of the Outer Amstel, so well drawn by Mr Rembrandt's own hand.' Rembrandt may not always have been alone on his walks.

If one turns back, as Rembrandt must have done when he made one of

his last landscape drawings, one gets a distant view of Amsterdam. Rembrandt suggests the movement of the fast-flowing river. It is one of those all too frequent days when the wind is blowing forcefully. The trees, the rushes, the sail of the boat, all yield to its pressure. On the right a man sits in a boat, behind him a second man dives into the river. In the immediate foreground a young man bends down to pick a flower or a plant. He interrupts our view and we resent his appearance, but he serves to give the scale to the scene, and also shows the human element reasserting itself in Rembrandt's art.

Once the Amstel reaches Ouderkerk, which contains the eerie Jewish cemetery known so well from Ruisdael's painting, the river becomes more open and there are fewer trees and houses. But to the north-east there is a small tributary known as the Bullewyk, along which Rembrandt made the drawing of a man rowing a boat. Behind there is one of his favourite motifs, a farm surrounded by trees, and how sensitively Rembrandt describes the function of the trees to shade from the sun and protect from the wind. Beyond in the distance is the spire of Ouderkerk Church. Here the river is narrower and more closed in. The water is more lethargic, the banks higher, with profuse rushes. It is more intimate landscape. Whereas the Amstel kept one on the move, here one is tempted to halt and rest.

Though the artist's favourite walks were along the Diemerdyke and the

90

89 *View of the Amstel with Amsterdam in the Background, c. 1655*

90 *A Man Rowing a Boat on the Bullewyk, c. 1650*

Amstel, they were not exclusively so. About 1651 Rembrandt made a trip to Haarlem. Outside the town, at the beginning of the dunes, there is a high point, still known as 'het Kopje', from which one gets a panoramic view back towards Haarlem and the flat country all round. It was the view from this spot which suggested the etching known by its traditional title of *The Goldweigher's Field*. That landmark of Haarlem, the spire of the Groote Kerk, can be seen in the distance on the left. (The scene is reversed in the print.) The church and houses of Bloemendaal are only partially camouflaged by the trees in the middle-ground. If the scene is off the artist's beaten track, there was a reason for the journey. On the left of the etching, Rembrandt has depicted a country house called Saxenburg, which at the time belonged to a certain Christoffel Thijsz. Thijsz was none other than one of the vendors of the artist's house in the Breestraat. Over ten years later the house was still far from paid for, and it may well be that this etching was intended as part payment.

91 *View outside Haarlem (The Goldweigher's Field)*, 1651

At an earlier date Rembrandt made a journey into eastern Holland, travelling as far as Arnhem on the Rhine, a favourite site for artists. Sketching tours – pleasant reminders of a leisurely existence – were common practice among other Dutch artists, but this is the only lengthy expedition Rembrandt allowed himself. It is tempting to believe that he went with his pupil Lambert Doomer, as has been suggested. Rembrandt has left us his impressions of Utrecht, Amersfoort, the ruined Church of Muiderberg, the hilly bushy landscape of Gelderland, and above all of Rhenen, the small town on the Rhine this side of Arnhem.

There are no less than four highly finished drawings of the old gateways 92 of Rhenen. One of them shows the inner gate on the west, or Utrecht Gate, seen from a point inside the town. The crumbling masonry and small dwellings clinging alongside the main structure of the gateway are evocative of age. The elaborate washes depict the different colours and textures. Yet though there are many shades of wash, they are all of one colour, for as has been said Rembrandt was a puritan where colour was concerned.

In Amersfoort he again chose the oldest part of the town, and drew the canal known as the Singel, near the well-known steeple. On both sides the back of houses and gardens border the water. There is a smell of stagnant water and picturesque decay.

The drawings made on this journey display a marked penchant for crumbling gateways, ruined and medieval churches, old houses bordering a canal. Though recent experiences may have encouraged this sentimental attitude towards the past, this taste illumines something more fundamental in Rembrandt's nature. At heart he was a conservative with a deep reverence for history. He would have agreed with Burke that 'Institutions contain the collective wisdom of ages.' One finds this attitude coming to the fore in every direction, whether in the nature of his collection, or the copies he made after other works of art, or in his sketches on his travels or in the home city. Fashion's habit of spurning the past was alien to his nature.

Amsterdam was matching its economic expansion with a similar increase in the size of the city. When Rembrandt arrived there in 1631, the phase of building, dominated by the figure of Hendrick de Keyser, was slowly losing impetus. About the middle of the century the country found

92 *The Western Gate at Rhenen, c.* 1648

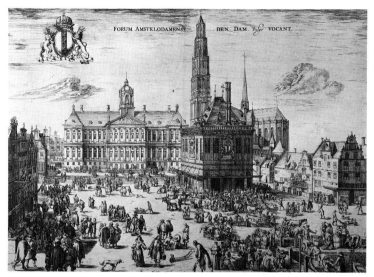

93 JACOB VAN DER ULFT *The New Town Hall and the Weighhouse, Amsterdam*

94 *The Old Town Hall of Amsterdam in Ruins, 1652*

a new source of inspiration in Italian architecture. Jacob van Campen was the most active exponent of the new style. Everything foreign was the order of the day and the new Town Hall in Amsterdam set the standard. A classical building, whose detail appears too small in scale for its immense size, replaced the old medieval Netherlandish Town Hall. The sculptors were Flemish, although the painters were mainly Dutch.

93

What did Rembrandt feel about this? He never drew the new Town Hall and it is hardly inapposite that his few connections with the building were anything but happy. Instead he made several drawings of the old Town Hall. The new building was begun in 1648 and as work proceeded they started to demolish the old Town Hall. But in 1652 part of the demolitions caught fire. Rembrandt made a drawing which he inscribed 'The Town Hall of Amsterdam after the fire of 9 July 1652, seen from the weighhouse'; the building stands in the foreground of Jacob van der Ulft's etching. Whereas the crowds gathered round to watch out of idle curiosity, Rembrandt made his drawing as an act of piety. It was for him *the* Town Hall, not the old Town Hall.

94

The same spirit asserts itself in the drawing Rembrandt made of the Montelbaarnstoren which formed part of the old fortifications. When the city outgrew the limits of the old ramparts, these towers became obsolete. But instead of being demolished they were transformed into belfries as ornaments to the city, which they remain. To complete the process the

95 ZEEMAN *The Montelbaarnstoren, Amsterdam*

96 *The Montelbaarnstoren, Amsterdam, c.* 1652

towers were capped with pointed roofs. The one added to the Montelbaarnstoren was done in the year of Rembrandt's birth; it can be seen in a drawing by Zeeman. Even though Rembrandt never knew the tower in its former state, he firmly ignored the later addition when he came to draw it; he also gave it a broader, less elegant base. The tower stands somewhat forlorn, but it still retains its character of a squat rugged fortification, a relic of the past.

About ten years after *The Night Watch* had been delivered Rembrandt returned to the site where it was hanging and drew the Kloveniersdoelen and the tower next to it, known in the seventeenth century as the Zwijgt-

97 *The Tower, Zwijgt-Utrecht,*
*and the Back of the Kloveniersdoelen,*
*Amsterdam, c.* 1655

98 Zeeman *The Old Pesthuis*
*outside Amsterdam*

99 *The Old Pesthuis or Fever*
*Hospital outside Amsterdam,*
*c.* 1655

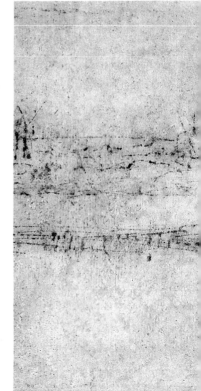

97 Utrecht. His view was probably taken from the bridge which crossed the Amstel a little farther up the river. Once again he restored his subject to its pristine shape. The spire and gable seen in the engraving might never have been added as far as Rembrandt was concerned.

One of the last landscape drawings Rembrandt made depicted the Old Pesthuis, or Fever Hospital, which lay on the south-west outskirts of the city, on the way to the small village of Den Overtoom. An etching by
98 Zeeman shows us the river in more detail. The mills on the city bulwarks
99 can be made out behind the Pesthuis, and in Rembrandt's drawing the tower of the Westerkerk, where Rembrandt was to be buried, appears on the left of the hospital. The Pesthuis had already appeared in one of Rembrandt's earliest landscape drawings. The wheel has come full circle. Here the building loses all substance and becomes a vision like a fully lit ship

100 *Holy Family in the Carpenter's Shop, c.* 1645

101 *Holy Family in the Carpenter's Shop*, 1645

102 *Jacob and Esau,*
*c.* 1648

sailing through the night. Only the man tramping towards his boat has any reality.

Simplicity and tranquillity create the predominant mood of the 1640s and are reflected in both style and subject matter. As has been seen landscape played an important part in this transformation, but at the same time as his activities in this field were starting there were already indications of new tendencies in his religious works of the later 1630s. The change was not the result of a spontaneous decision but was gradually evolved over a number of years so that new interests appear alongside the old. Around 1640 the different trends can be seen concurrently in the same work. There 77 is still a great deal of the earlier Baroque style in *The Night Watch* of 1642, whereas the more intimate and homely are already apparent in certain 49 details of the etching of the *Death of the Virgin* of three years earlier.

A change in subject matter, invariably an essential ingredient in Rembrandt's work, is soon noticeable. Gone is the taste for demonstrations of strength and display in favour of simpler moments in the life of Christ

103 *The Sacrifice of Isaac,* 1645

such as the *Holy Family in the Carpenter's Shop.* It is not without significance 101 that two further pictures, to be discussed later, in the series for the Stadholder, illustrate scenes from Christ's infancy rather than his Passion. In his choice of themes from the Old Testament Rembrandt picks out reflective moments indicative of inner character and quiet emotion. He develops a penchant for incidents involving two participants, whose psychological interaction is conveyed by an intense concentration on feeling or thought produced by a harmony of form. To provide a focal point he often employs the gesture of a hand or hands. In a drawing of *Jacob and Esau,* the motif of the clasped hands as the brothers seal their agreement both unites them and provides the clue to that particular story. When Rembrandt had painted the *Sacrifice of Isaac* in 1635, he had taken delight in the outward manifestations of the miracle to the extent that he depicts the knife released from Abraham's hand suspended incongruously in mid-air. Returning to the theme in an etching ten years later, he now concentrates on expressing the warring emotions of a loving father at odds with those of _an obedient servant of God. The angel no longer appears, and Abraham's pointing hand links the interplay of emotion between father and son.

In both works style is moulded to achieve the artist's purpose. Both in outline and modelling the figures are conceived separately, providing each with its own identity in a more classical mode. The composition is treated in the manner of a bas-relief so that the shallow space projects the figures against the background unified by parallel shading, whose function he probably studied in the engravings of Andrea Mantegna. Chiaroscuro is much less obvious and is employed in small areas especially over the face in order to create that sense of the inner person.

101    Probably the most outstanding painting of the period is the *Holy Family in the Carpenter's Shop* of 1645, in which Rembrandt succeeds in combining the miraculous and the homely found in the etching of the *Death of the Virgin* to obtain a new level of poetic spirituality. Were it not for the appearance of the angels through the window there would be little, apart from some idealization of the Virgin's face, to distinguish the subject from a genre scene of a carpenter preoccupied with his trade, while his wife, seated beside the fire, looks up from her book towards the baby in the cradle. It is a spectacle of humble intimacy wrapped in a veil of mystery, which demonstrates Rembrandt's mastery in elevating the everyday into a specific emotional experience. The underlying structure of the

100    composition is revealed in a brilliant schematic study of the kind more often to be found in the work of Rubens than Rembrandt. In remarkably few lines Rembrandt adumbrates the figures and unequivocally establishes their positions in the four different planes of the composition, at the same time suggesting the play of light. The Virgin and child in the cradle are hardly identifiable as objects, but their relationship to one another is unmistakably articulated. Following his drawing, Rembrandt portrays the interior in a magical play of light and half-shadows, incorporating such realistic details as the cradle and the fire within the prevailing atmosphere of heightened spirituality. Brushstrokes are designed to convey colour, form and texture within the prevailing tone. The colours, red, green, gold and brown, act in quiet sympathy yet provide sufficient variety.

If everything is perfectly harmonized in this picture, another work vividly shows the quest for a new style. The large print generally known as

104    the *Hundred Guilder Print* illustrates various incidents of Christ's ministry described in chapter 19 of St Matthew's Gospel. The stylistically different features and the manifold alterations made to the plate point to a lengthy period of execution, possibly from 1639 until ten years later. Rembrandt may have seen his struggle with this work primarily in terms of technique in order to create a simpler, more monumental effect by blending etching

104 *The Hundred Guilder Print*, *c.* 1639–49

and drypoint. But no less visible are the artist's modifications of subject. The initial conception was grandiose with a vast cast skilfully arranged around the central figure of Christ, in a manner reminiscent of the painting of *St John Preaching*. But as he worked on the plate he developed another side to the subject. Such incidents as the woman approaching Christ and the figure of the rich young man pondering his predicament largely or wholly date from the end of his work. At the same time the chiaroscuro was infinitely varied to heighten individual figures or incidents yet create an overall pattern which radiates from the central figure of Christ. Such lengthy and intense work on one plate must have caused the artist much frustration and anguish, but it is characteristic of Rembrandt's slow determination that he never abandoned it. And his successful conclusion allowed him a freedom and mastery of etching in the future. From another point of view this work can be seen as the eventual triumph over a stylistic problem occurring in the middle of an artist's career.

50

125

## CHAPTER FOUR

## New patrons and new Companions

At Saskia's death Titus was no more than one year old. Both Saskia's sister Titia and Rembrandt's mother were dead and there was no one in the immediate family circle to step in and help. Clearly a nurse was required, but in view of the outcome and what it revealed of Rembrandt's character, the choice was unfortunate. He picked on a trumpeter's widow by the name of Geertge Dircx. She is traditionally identified with the drawing of a peasant in the local costume of Waterland in north Holland, which is inscribed on the back in a contemporary hand: 'the nurse of Titus'. Houbraken describes her as 'a little farm woman . . . rather small of person but well made in appearance and plump of body'. From subsequent events it is evident that she became Rembrandt's common law wife, and he rashly gave her jewellery, which had belonged to Saskia, and which included a valuable rose ring set with diamonds and an uninscribed 'marriage medallion'. It was ill luck for Geertge that another woman, Hendrickje Stoffels, entered Rembrandt's household in the 1640s and supplanted the former in the artist's affections. The *menage à trois* became intolerable and in 1649 Geertge was ousted from the house. She retaliated by taking Rembrandt before the Chamber of Matrimonial Cases to answer a breach of promise suit, citing as evidence the gift of the ring as a pledge and the fact that he had slept with her on a number of occasions. After various charges and counter-charges and two instances of Rembrandt's refusal to appear before the court, Geertge was awarded an annuity of 200 guilders for life, which may in the end have seemed a worthwhile price to be rid of her, although it amounted to twenty-five per cent more than Rembrandt had originally offered.

But that was far from being the end of the affair since Geertge still retained the jewellery which, undoubtedly at Rembrandt's insistence, she had left to Titus in a will drawn up in 1648. But as soon she left the artist's house she began to pawn the jewellery and continued to do so even after the court's judgment in her favour. With Rembrandt's connivance if not at his direct instigation, a sufficiently convincing case, for reasons now unknown, was brought against her in 1650 in order to sentence her to a reformatory. The artist paid for her transportation to the house of

105 *Geertge Dircx(?)*,
*c.* 1645

correction in Gouda and the following year tried to see that she was detained for a further eleven years. And in 1655 in a vivid encounter, recorded in a document, he attempted to prevent a friend of Geertge obtaining her release after five years' incarceration. The woman called on Rembrandt on her way to Gouda; when told of her intention he replied that 'he did not think she would do such a thing, and shaking his finger at her and threatening: "if you go, you will regret it"'. Despite his following up these words with letters of protest to Gouda, Geertge was released and went home to her native Waterland. Her name only occurs once again in connection with Rembrandt, when ironically she was listed amongst his creditors in his declaration of insolvency in 1656.

Rembrandt's representative before the court in 1649 was Hendrickje Stoffels, who was a sergeant's daughter from Bredevoort. This is the first mention of her and establishes, as has been seen, that she was already a

127

106 *A Woman Bathing*, 1654

member of the artist's household. She was to remain there until her death, assuming Saskia's role in all but name. Rembrandt's failure to marry her may have been partly due to the terms of Saskia's will, since he would have lost the income from her part of the estate, which with his house still unpaid for he could not afford. But as also in the case of Geertge Dircx, it might have been socially unacceptable for the artist to marry someone from such a humble background. Nevertheless, his reluctance caused him a lot of annoyance. At the very height of his financial troubles he talked of remarrying. Two years before, in 1654, the Council of the Reformed Church summoned Hendrickje three times but she paid no attention. At the fourth summons she appeared before them and admitted that 'she had stained herself by fornication with Rembrandt', for which she was punished, urged to repent and forbidden from taking communion. Three months later their natural child, Cornelia, was baptized in the Oude Kerk. Thereafter the church left Hendrickje in peace.

Faced with the problem of widowerhood, Rubens for all his numerous friends and constant travelling still felt, as he so memorably expressed himself, the lack of those attentions that only a woman can give. He chose 'a young wife of honest but middle-class family'. Undoubtedly Rembrandt felt the same, but his need may have been greater, for taciturnity increased with age. As well as needing a 'mother' for Titus and a wife for himself, he required someone who would understand his moods and provide him with silent companionship. Despite the opulent bourgeois life-style he and Saskia established, he now deliberately sought an unassuming and undemanding consort from a lower class. The explanation offered by the French writer André de Piles (1699) may contain more than a germ of the truth: 'He loved to keep mean company. Some of his friends told him of it, to whom he answered: "When I have a mind to unbend and recreate my mind, I do not care so much for honour as I do for liberty."'

With their apparent community of temperaments but opposition of backgrounds, Saskia must have been a stimulant to Rembrandt. She was no doubt what he wished he had been born. One suspects their life together was not always serene. With his change of mood Rembrandt required a softer, more compliant partner. Hendrickje was the perfect answer. Her simpler background may not have given her the art of conversation, but, intuitively, she could admire and understand him. She played a more basic role in the house, whereas Saskia had probably been more of an adornment. The little existing contemporary opinion of Hendrickje records her as a loving mother and an affectionate and loyal companion.

Just as Saskia had, so Hendrickje provided the ever convenient model. She slipped into Rembrandt's life in an unconventional way so that he

107 *Self-portrait, holding his Palette, Brushes and Maulstick, c. 1663*

108 *Self-portrait*, 1658

109 *Titus drawing at a Desk, c.* 1655

110 *Women sewing in the Artist's House, c.* 1655

never made the formal portrait as he did with Saskia. Her role must have slowly and unobtrusively changed from servant and nurse to wife. Her face, or a distillation of it, appears in so many works, yet it is nearly always difficult to be certain that it is she who is represented. She was a model not a sitter. More often than not we can only guess that she inspired the work. The drawing of a woman looking out of a window may well depict her. Such a contemplative study would fit her character. She was quieter, more slow moving than Saskia, with none of the latter's coquettish nature.

Equally unsubstantiated is the identification of Hendrickje as the subject of the small painting of a *Woman bathing*, which beautifully exemplifies the 106 artist's freedom of execution in a work which rates as more than an oil sketch yet cannot be regarded as a finished work in the conventional sense, even if the artist chose to sign and date it. An attractive, plumpish woman, who carefully lifts up her chemise, stands in the stream, looking down completely absorbed in her own thoughts. It might have been intended as a Biblical subject, but the artist offers us no clue. We gain the impression that the artist painted the panel directly before the model, brilliantly contrasting the fluidly modelled soft flesh with the bold spontaneous brushstrokes of

111 *Hendrickje(?) looking out of the Window, c.* 1655

112 *Danaë*, 1636

white describing the chemise. Its very discretion in its lack of revelation of
the intimate parts of the body makes it the more sensuous. Only the
background was probably painted in afterwards to envelop the figure in an
atmosphere of dark shadows and sumptuous colour. The rich gold and red
garments are piled together on the river bank, with the reflection of the
latter colour staining the water. The picture's harmonious hermetic world
may offer a clue to the relationship between artist and model.

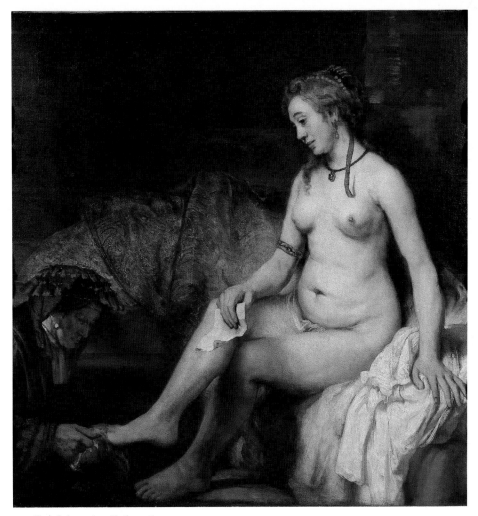

113 *Bathsheba at her Toilet,* 1654

Titus also played his part as model and there are a number of works which show him engaged in all the usual occupations of a boy of his age: sleeping, writing, thinking, poring over books, or sitting at a desk drawing. It is hardly a surprise he took up his father's profession, even if he left no more than a few mediocre works. 109

Life must have continued normally in the house in the Breestraat, or so it would appear from a drawing made at this time. On the left three women on stools sit busy sewing, while another woman sits in a high-backed chair on the right. Doubtless they gossiped as they worked, though their chatter flowed over the head of the artist hard at work. In the background can be seen the same fireplace with caryatids which was depicted in the drawing of Saskia on her sickbed.

Rembrandt's self-portraits cover the whole of his life, but they reach a new peak during the last twenty years. One of the most monumental is the painting dated 1652. The artist, dressed in a painting tunic, stands facing us, with his hands placed firmly on his hips. In a drawing which may be a preparatory study, he represents himself full length but though he reduced it to three-quarter length on canvas he loses nothing in melancholy intensity. There is something uncompromising about his stare. Baldinucci wrote that 'the ugly and plebeian face by which he was ill-favoured, was accompanied by untidy and dirty clothes, since it was his custom, when working, to wipe his brushes on himself, and to do other things of a similar nature. When he worked he would not have granted an audience to the first monarch in the world, who would have had to return again and again until he found him no longer engaged on that work.'

Rembrandt's purpose in producing so many self-portraits and how they are to be interpreted remain two of the most puzzling problems of his painting. In the first examples he had used himself as the most readily available model for a whole range of studies in facial expression. After his move to Amsterdam his self-portraits tended to vary between 'costume-pieces' in which he adorned himself in fanciful headgear and clothing and the intensely serious self-analysis painted in 1640. After a gap in the 1640s, he returned with renewed vigour to the genre and during the last two decades of his life carried out a greater number and variety than previously. Moreover, because of their human grandeur we are inclined to accord them greater significance.

Although no other artist matched Rembrandt's output, self-portraiture flourished in the seventeenth century. It fell into two general types: either the artist was depicted without any attributes or he was represented as a member of his profession, often accompanied by statuary, books and musical and scientific instruments, all of which stressed the noble status of the artist. With some variations Rembrandt followed these two modes, although attributes are restricted and the focus is invariably on the face and its expression. The majority belong to the first category, but he invariably rings the changes with the formal arrangement and mood, as in the paintings of 1652, 1657 and 1669. There are several works in which he depicts himself with the tools of his profession, but unlike some other artists the latter are strictly limited to what he needed to paint and included none

136

114 *Self-portrait*, 1652

of those symbols of learning. In no work does he present himself more
107 magisterially than in the picture of about 1663 with its uncompromising frontal position. He holds his palette, brushes and maulstick, and is dressed in working clothes with a white cap on his head. On the wall behind are two mysterious circles, whose inclusion may have been prompted by the basic circular pattern of contemporary world maps which were sometimes used as wall decoration in houses. These establish a breadth to the design and provide a counterbalance to the triangular shape of the massively realized figure. The simple geometrical shapes underlying the picture concentrate the eye on the face with its searingly direct gaze and austere mood expressed by the limited range of sombre colouring.

Some five years before in an equally monumental work he returns to the
108 kind of 'costume-piece' he produced in earlier years. Seated on a chair, three-quarter length, he is dressed in oriental garments with a large flat cap on his head. The resigned unsmiling expression, habitually without a trace of self-pity, contrasts with the unparalleled richness of colour; glowing gold and red stand out from a range of browns, all brought into harmony by the application of glazes. In another self-portrait he appears as the ageing
115 St Paul. And in one of the most extraordinary works executed at the very end of his life he shows himself laughing. Various interpretations have been proffered, but it may represent Zeuxis, the painter of legendary fame who, according to Van Mander, 'departed this life laughing immoderately, choking while painting a funny wrinkled old woman in the flesh'. Although the latter is not now identifiable, there is evidence that the painting has been cut. (A complete representation of the theme occurs in a painting by his pupil Aert de Gelder). If correctly interpreted it offers another self-identification with an artist of the past.

Confronted with such a unique range of images of psychological concentration and overpowering individuality, we ask ourselves how far we are justified in relating the mood of each picture with the events of the artist's life. Although parallels between the two can reasonably be made, it is no less feasible that as an aid to his study of humanity he returned to his earlier practice of using himself as model. However we answer this question it is a fact that his self-portraits, which constitute a substantial part of his oeuvre – some fifty exist today – were barely mentioned by any seventeenth-century writer and only very occasionally can be identified in collections of the period. And none were described in the inventory of the artist's own possessions.

In the same inventory the room on the second floor in the front of the house in the Breestraat was described as the 'large studio' ('groote Schilderkamer'). This must be the room which appears in one of the many

115 *Self-portrait laughing, c.* 1668

116 *A Model in the Artist's Studio, c.* 1655

drawings of the nude done in the 1650s. On the left the artist sits working, hidden by the easel. At the other side of the room a model, nude to the waist, sits on a stool facing a home-made desk. The lower half of the window has been covered so that the artist has a strong top light.

Like landscape the nude played an intermittent but essential part in Rembrandt's work. Studied in both drawings and etchings at three specific moments in his career, the nude developed as much into a subject in its own right as a preparation for appropriate figures in religious and mythological subjects. Despite following the Renaissance tradition of working from the nude, Rembrandt was consistently unacademic, and in his first examples

117 *Naked Woman on a Mound, c.* 1631

seems to have gone out of his way to assert his independence. Although
Rubens' work in general and Annibale Carracci's etching of *Susanna and the
Elders* in particular have been adduced as prototypes for Rembrandt's
etching of a *Naked Woman on a Mound*, the last offers a slice of unadorned
reality lacking the degree of grace and idealism in the works of the two
older artists. The 'washerwoman' or 'treader of peat from the barn', as a
later seventeenth-century Dutch writer referred to the model, is virtually
studied as an anatomical specimen, the shock effect of which is only muted
by the chiaroscuro.

Although substantially repainted at a later date, the *Danaë* of 1636 is the    112

118 *Reclining Female Nude, c.* 1646

nearest equivalent to the classical nude in the Titian tradition. Produced at his most Baroque period, the picture is characteristically rich in incident, detail and colour, all devised to reveal the sensuous nude from her cocoon of shadow. But even in this work Rembrandt introduces an element of individuality in his portrayal of the nude at odds with the classical ideal. Hung beside a *Venus* by Titian, the *Danaë* would assert itself more forcefully by virtue of the element of reality.

In his second phase of studying the nude in the mid-1640s, Rembrandt made a number of drawings and etchings. In a beautiful black chalk drawing of a reclining female nude Rembrandt makes no attempt to follow the classical ideal. She reminds us of the description of Geertge, 'rather small of person but well made in appearance and plump of body'. The drawing differs from earlier examples by its insistence, by means of outline and modelling, on the form of the body, heightened in this example by the application of white bodycolour to the highlights. One etching of the male nude may have been drawn largely before the model. Two separate studies are composed by an imaginary band of shadow, while a lightly bitten genre scene of a woman teaching a child to walk is added in the background. In these studies Rembrandt achieves a remarkable balance which allows us to

19

apprehend the weight and continuity of the forms of the body while the play of light avoids the effect of an academic study in a vacuum.

During the 1650s Rembrandt once again took up the theme of the female nude. His most searching analysis was done in drawing, which with the landscapes and Biblical subjects constitutes the most extensive part of his later work in the medium. Whereas he had previously used chalk for the most part, he now worked exclusively with the reed pen and the tip of the brush, sometimes with the addition of wash. No longer was he interested in the rendering of flesh or the delineation of form, but was entirely concerned with a monumental image of the female figure, created by an abstract equivalent rather than a conventional outline. In one of his most summary studies of the reclining nude, the soft open lines of the reed pen realize the essence of form without distracting detail. And to complement his study, a few calculated touches of wash indicate the fall of light over the figure and background. The theme of the female figure suffused in the light and atmosphere of its setting was most consistently developed in the six etchings he made between 1658 and 1661. In his rendering of the figure he followed the same principles as in his drawings by a combination of

120

119 *Young Man seated, Another standing, c.* 1646

drypoint and deeply etched lines. The indeterminate setting encumbered with few accessories was created out of a varied web of parallel shading. One etching is devoted to a model sitting with her feet in a bathtub, a hat on the chair beside her. But what lifts this simple study out of the ordinary is the effect of light cast onto part of the body and the background, which are separated by a world of flickering shadows. And to assist him to obtain the desired result, he often printed with surface tone on oriental papers.

This intensive study of the nude led to only one painting executed in 1654 at the very beginning of his activity. Admittedly one might claim that it said in paint all that was necessary. In its highly personal way, the nude, which is more fully modelled than in the drawings, is not only beautiful in itself but is used as a means of expressing the essential element in the story of David's infatuation. At the same time Rembrandt portrays the touching humanity of Bathsheba's demeanour as she ponders her answer. Two very different centres of interest, the face and the body, are miraculously balanced within a setting of glowing colour and warm chiaroscuro. The pose of Bathsheba and the old woman drying her feet may well have been derived from a classical relief, which appropriately represents a bride before her wedding night. This source possibly assisted Rembrandt in creating the aura of calm and tectonic scale expressed as much in the nude itself as in the whole composition.

When studying the nude, Rembrandt did not always work alone and on occasions he would hold a life class for his pupils. A pupil shows us such a

121

113

*120 Reclining Nude, c. 1659*

121 *Woman at the Bath with a Hat beside her,* 1658

122

class in progress. The master corrects one pupil's drawing; another listens in to his advice; a third puts his drawing at a distance to measure its progress. Others get on with their work of drawing the nude model, who stands on the right on a throne. Another pupil's drawing of a similar scene includes a row of plaster casts, which were clearly used for copying.

Rembrandt's words as a teacher have not come down to us directly but sufficient can be learnt from a treatise written by one of his pupils, Samuel van Hoogstraten, in conjunction with drawings by the master and pupils to

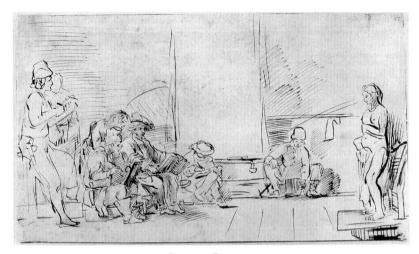

determine the general nature of his instruction. Characteristically Rembrandt was unorthodox in his procedure and largely broke away from the traditional guild system of apprenticeship, which involved a rigid and lengthy programme, starting with the menial tasks of grinding colours and preparing canvasses. (As we have seen, Rembrandt did follow the practice of making pupils copy his works, which were then put up for sale.) Instead Rembrandt established a private academy, in which instruction was offered on a far less formal basis, so that some students worked under him for a number of years while others enrolled for much shorter periods. This system ultimately derived from the academy set up by the Carracci family in Bologna to promote the study of nature and classical art. A rather similar organization appears to have been run by Carel van Mander, Hendrick Goltzius and Cornelis van Haarlem in Haarlem at the end of the sixteenth century, although the 'famosa accademia' of Van Ulenborch, in which Rembrandt himself may have participated, was probably a more relevant factor in determining the latter's practice.

The traditional Renaissance programme consisted of instruction in anatomy and perspective, drawings from casts and the nude, and copying works of the master and other artists. With one important distinction Rembrandt, whose teaching echoed his own methods of working, used the same system. Life drawing is documented not only by the two drawings of sessions in progress, but also by a number of nude studies of the same model seen from different angles, undoubtedly the work of the master and pupils at the same sitting. (The model in question was the young man who was the subject of the etching of 1646.) But as Rembrandt's own studies 119 demonstrate neither anatomical correctness nor the use of perspective was paramount. Moreover, the corrections which he was in the habit of making to pupils' drawings, whether of the nude or some other subject, were directed solely towards enhancing the expression of the subject. It was this aspect of his teaching which shocked that strict classicist, Sandrart, who wrote that Rembrandt 'did not hesitate to oppose and contradict our rules of art, such as anatomy and the proportions of the human body, perspective and the usefulness of classical statues, Raphael's drawing and judicious pictorial disposition, and the academies which are so particularly necessary for our profession. . . . As circumstances demanded, he approved in a picture light and shade and the outline of objects, even if in contradiction with the simple fact of the horizon, as long as in his opinion they were successful and apposite.'

123 *Satire on Art Criticism*, 1644

Although Rembrandt taught his students to work in his style, this was only part of the programme and not the ultimate goal. Unlike Rubens, who employed a number of apprentices and assistants, Rembrandt never or very rarely used his pupils to help him with his own paintings or etchings. After being grounded in Rembrandt's manner, they were, therefore, encouraged to develop their own artistic personalities, and the unprecedented use of cubicles mentioned earlier was presumably introduced for this purpose. Having finished their training, some pupils went their own way, more often than not adopting the more fashionable style of the time, while others continued to work in Rembrandt's manner. Given the originality and strength of the latter's own work, it is hardly surprising that some found it difficult to establish their own independence. Houbraken records that Govaert Flinck, for example, had problems in escaping. It may be as much a reflection on the master himself for all his liberal system that none of his pupils became a major artist.

123    If there remain some uncertainties about Rembrandt's teaching, there are none about his opinions on art connoisseurship. In one drawing the critic sits on a barrel pontificating. With the familiarity of an old hand, he points to a picture with his pipe. Attribution, subject, and date, not just the year but the very month, we can be sure, fall glibly from his mouth. His ass's ears are noticed by none of the eager crowd agog for the next piece of expertise. One picture lies rejected on the ground. Another is being brought forward. Only the man on the lower right is unimpressed. It is a satire that has lost none of its bite.

It is too easy to suggest that Rembrandt's life was a perpetual *andante maestoso*. Money was short, and the fashionable commissions now went to the artists who were prepared to paint in the new Flemish manner. His former pupils, Bol and Flinck, were among those who took over his clientele. But Rembrandt still had his friends and clients. Far more exclusively they are drawn from the professional class, preachers, doctors, and occasional fellow-artists. But there were two predominant exceptions, who provided him with work.

Frederick Henry was evidently still pleased with his five paintings of scenes from the Passion and only a year or two before he died he had ordered two more. His account book lists a payment to Rembrandt in 1646 for 2,400 guilders for a *Nativity* and a *Circumcision*. Two years before Rembrandt's death the series was described as 'seven paintings done by Rembrandt, all in black frames, with oval top and encircled by gilt and
124    foliage'. Only one of the additional two exists today, *The Nativity*, or more accurately, *The Adoration of the Shepherds*. Though the same size as the original five, it is painted on canvas instead of panel. A more important

148

124 *The Adoration of the Shepherds, 1646*

change is the much greater intimacy and quietness. Of the earlier pictures, only *The Entombment* had something of this mood.

If the Stadholder had a specialist knowledge of technique he would have been aware of the changes in Rembrandt's method of painting from his earlier works. The handling of the brush lost its previous primary function of defining form and modelling, as well as indicating movement and texture. Now the strokes were more broadly applied in open juxtaposition to one another so that tone and form are now suggested rather than described. Unlike the smooth finish of the first works in the series, no attempt was made to merge changes of tone and colour apart from the application of glazes, which enriched the surface. Each picture was deliberately designed to read correctly only from a distance. The seven pictures stretching in date of execution over thirteen years offered an excellent paradigm of Rembrandt's growing mastery in the actual process of painting.

An equally important figure in Rembrandt's life during these years was Jan Six, but although there is abundant proof of his patronage, there is little direct evidence to uphold the eighteenth-century legend that they were intimate friends. There are no letters between the two men and there are no indications how their relationship developed, although they had a number of artistic interests in common.

Jan Six, who was twelve years Rembrandt's junior, came of a family of Huguenot refugees. His grandfather, the youngest son of a noble family in St Omer, had fled to Amsterdam, where he set up as a dyer and merchant. Six's father died early but the business was taken over by his widow, Anna Wijmer, who also supervised her son's education at Leiden University followed by the Grand Tour in Italy in 1640. As happens in successful families, the son's heart was not in business, although to begin with he played some part in the direction of the family dye-works and silk mills.

His interests lay elsewhere in the fields of art, literature and learning and he soon acquired a reputation as a dilettante and poet. It is thus rather than as a businessman that Rembrandt portrayed him for the first time. The etching of 1647 shows Six standing by the window reading. There is a painting on the wall (its curtain allows us to see only a few figures), and a pile of books on the chair. The sitter is lost in thought, as if meditating on some Classical tragedy. Unusually for Rembrandt, we possess three working drawings, which disclose the initial intention of presenting the sitter as a country gentleman, resting his elbow on the window sill and looking directly out at the spectator. A dog jumps up at his side and there is no sign of any books in the room. We unfortunately do not know whether the change to a more bookish reflective portrait was due to sitter or artist.

125 *Jan Six*, 1647

126 *Medea, or the Marriage of Jason and Creusa*, 1648

Equally unusual in this work was the very high degree of finish obtained by a combination of etching and drypoint, which succeeds in equalling the tonal richness of the newly discovered technique of mezzotint. Only the space through the window and the reflected light on Six's face are at the top end of the light scale; the remainder of the plate is depicted in a thousand shades of grey and black. That the result met with critical acclaim at the time is attested by a projected portrait commission which, according to the contract, 'the forenamed Rijn shall etch from the life, to be of the quality of the portrait of Heer van Six'.

Six moved in the best intellectual circles. He consorted with both Spinoza and Descartes. His first long poem was dedicated to Pieter Cornelisz. Hooft, the reigning deity of the Muiden circle. He became a close friend of Vondel. The latter and Rembrandt probably met, but no

127 *Jan Six writing at his Estate at Ijmond(?), c. 1655*

intimacy developed. Although Vondel wrote extensively about other artists, Rembrandt's name rarely occurs, and then only in poems attached to portraits following the custom of the time.

The year after Rembrandt's portrait etching, Six published another long poem, a tragedy entitled *Medea*, a copy of which later belonged to Rembrandt. He invited the latter to contribute an etching to be used as a frontispiece to the volume. Following contemporary practice of enlivening a piece lacking in action, Rembrandt, presumably with the agreement of the author, illustrates a scene which does not occur in Six's tragedy at all. His etching shows Medea appearing at the wedding of Jason and Creusa. In one hand she bears a 'gift' of poison and in the other a dagger. As in the case of other etchings Rembrandt did as illustrations, only a few copies of the book contain them. However, Rembrandt stubbornly refused to accept the fact that etching was an unsuitable medium for mass reproduction.

In 1652 Six abandoned business. The same year Rembrandt made two drawings in Six's 'Album Amicorum'. The first depicted *Homer reciting* and was suitably inscribed below 'Rembrandt aan Johannes Six'. Six, who increasingly in his later years was an enthusiastic admirer of Italian art, would not have let Rembrandt's debt to Raphael's *Parnassus* go

128 *St John the Baptist preaching, c.* 1655

unappreciated. Perhaps the choice of subject was a compliment, none too serious, one hopes, to his friend. On another page, Rembrandt made a drawing sometimes identified as a portrait of Six's mother as *Pallas Athene in her Study*, or more recently as a study of Minerva containing an implied compliment to Anna Wijmer's wisdom.

The following year Six lent Rembrandt the substantial sum of 1,000 guilders, although later for reasons undisclosed he asked for the money back, and when Rembrandt was unable to pay sold the debt at a discount to a third party. It was a loan which was to haunt the artist for a number of years to come. Six owned a small estate at Jaaphannes, which was situated on the Diemerdyke, where so many of Rembrandt's landscapes were drawn. A drawing of a man, whose features are hidden by his hat, as he sits writing, includes an identifiable view through the window of the River Y with Spaarndam on the far bank, and it may be that it represents a study of Six at his country home.

Six was a keen collector, and at his death owned numerous paintings and drawings by Dutch and Italian artists, as well as antique marbles, engraved

127

129 ANON. *Etching after Rembrandt's Jan Six,* 19th century

stones and other *objets d'art.* The character of his collection in many ways resembles Rembrandt's, and they would have found much in common to discuss on the subject. Among works by Rembrandt belonging to Six were a *Portrait of Saskia in a Red Hat* and the *St John the Baptist preaching,* both of which were the subject of a contract between the two men in 1652 but which was mysteriously annulled six years later. The latter picture, already discussed previously, was described in Six's sale catalogue as 'curious and artistic in the highest degree'. Presumably it needed a frame and about this time Rembrandt made a design, possibly inspired by a theatre proscenium arch, in which the details of the picture are only summarily sketched in.

The culmination of Rembrandt's relationship with Six was reached in the portrait painted in 1654, in which the latter is shown standing, head on one side, pulling on a glove. He is fashionably dressed in a long grey buttoned coat with a gold braided red cloak thrown casually over one shoulder. It offers a remarkable example of outstanding technique and portrait interpretation blended into a great work of art. The momentary action of pulling on a glove is carefully counterbalanced by the sober,

155

reflective mood. The eyes, partly hidden by the shadows cast from the brim of the hat, gain in depth and introspection, serving to create one of the most powerful representations of 'thinking man'. The mystery as to what he may be thinking is enhanced by the shadowy background from which the figure emerges. The painting of the face is carefully built up to convey the solidity of the head, yet the open strokes suggest the life beneath the outer skin. The virtuoso brushwork of the hands, in strokes which summarize rather than describe, establish an absorbing secondary centre of interest in the lower part of the canvas. It succeeds in being both a formal portrait recording the outer image of the man for posterity, yet informal in its complete absence of conscious posing. To record his complete satisfaction with the result, Six composed a Latin chronogram, inscribed in one of his albums: 'Such a face had I, Jan Six, who since childhood have worshipped the Muses'.

The picture marks the last certain contact between the painter and sitter. The next year Six married the daughter of Nicolaas Tulp. Rembrandt was never invited to paint her. That honour was given to his estranged pupils of earlier days, Bol and Flinck. The following year, which saw Rembrandt's financial crash, Six was nominated Commissioner of Marriages, his first step on the ladder of city service which was to lead to a spell as Burgomaster. But this peak was reached long after Rembrandt's death.

What happened to their relationship? Following the general trend in Holland, Six's taste became more classical in later years. A book of etchings by Jan de Bisschop after classical sculpture and Italian works of art was dedicated to him. The foreword contained a hardly concealed slighting reference to Rembrandt, lamenting the state of Dutch art which had to represent a Leda or Danaë with the figure of a charwoman. Divergence of taste apart, it may well be that Rembrandt with his increasing financial problems, not made more palatable by Six's request for the return of the loan, withdrew into his own private world, finding himself out of step with an ever more successful patrician.

Relations with other patrons were more straightforward if not as extensive. Among these was the Portuguese Jew Ephraim Bonus, who practised as a physician in Amsterdam. He was also a writer, who supported Menasseh ben Israel's Jewish publishing firm and the latter may well have been responsible for introducing him to Rembrandt. In a portrait etching made by Lievens, Bonus appears a well-fed successful doctor. Rembrandt in his print of 1647 makes him thoughtful, with a tinge of melancholy as he stops at the foot of the stairs, lost in reflection. With an infinite number of small strokes with the etching needle on the face, Rembrandt emphasizes the eyes and the hint of introspection. As in his

130 *Artistotle contemplating the Bust of Homer*, 1653

131 *Ephraim Bonus*, 1647

portrait etching of Six made in the same year, Rembrandt severely restricts the areas of highlight, building up the varied dark tones with a web of hatching. Apart from the lack of colour, it represents painting in etching, but unlike earlier examples it is produced in the latter's own language.

132    Another member of the medical fraternity who was in touch with Rembrandt was Arnold Tholinx. He was Inspector of the Medical Colleges in Amsterdam. By marriage he was related to Jan Six and Nicolaas Tulp, and he lived next door to the latter in a house on the Keizersgracht. But his connections with the artist did not stop there because he succeeded in his job by Johannes Deyman. In the very same year Rembrandt painted and probably etched Tholinx's portrait, he painted his *Anatomy Lesson of Dr Deyman*. Can it have been fortuitous that they both commissioned Rembrandt in the same year?

132 *Arnold Tholinx, c.* 1656

133 *Jan Asselyn, c.* 1647

134 *Clement de Jonghe,* 1651

135 *Jan Lutma the Elder,* 1656

136 *The Anatomy Lesson of Dr Johan Deyman*, 1656

The painting of Tholinx is limited to head and shoulders, whereas the etching was enlarged to portray the man in his setting. In order to suggest the character of the sitter, Rembrandt unlike so many of his contemporaries invariably created a different *mise-en-scène* for each portrait print. Here the sitter, pince-nez in hand, is seated at a table before his books, looking out at the spectator, the upper part of his face shaded by the wide brim of his hat. This print is especially notable for the beautiful play of reflected light over the face contrasted with the rich black shadows produced by an extensive use of drypoint.

Rembrandt had few close contacts with fellow-painters. His pupils either moved into a more fashionable milieu, as did Bol, Backer, and Flinck, or returned to their native town. Dordrecht claimed the return of Maes and Samuel van Hoogstraeten. Gerbrand van Eeckhout, who worked in the master's studio in the late 1630s, was among the few to keep up intimate relations. Houbraken describes Roelant Roghman, the landscape artist, as a 'great friend' of Rembrandt. A former non-pupil artist friend was Jan van de Capelle, a wealthy amateur painter of seascapes, who had some five hundred drawings by Rembrandt in his collection. He also had his portrait painted by him, but it no longer exists.

Another artist who was portrayed by Rembrandt is Jan Asselyn, who was probably a friend. In later years his brother, a poet, acted as Rembrandt's witness. Asselyn painted Italianate landscapes far removed from Rembrandt's style, and had returned from Italy probably the year before Rembrandt etched him. He was very small and his deformed hand gave rise to his nickname Crabbetje ('Little Crab'). His stature and deformity are carefully hidden as he sits or stands at his desk with a painting on the easel behind him, yet Rembrandt somehow conveys the look of a little man. In a later stage of the etching he removed the easel and painting so that the figure of the sitter stands out against a white background. The result is less successful, although it may enhance the sitter's stature. 133

In the same professional circles Rembrandt had contacts with the well-known printseller and publisher in Amsterdam Clement de Jonghe, who lived in the Calverstraat just near the Town Hall. De Jonghe published prints after Rembrandt and the inventory of his possessions gives the first descriptive list in any quantity of Rembrandt's etchings. Rembrandt portrayed him in an etching, which is remarkable for the increasing intensity he gave his sitter as the print progresses from state to state. 134

Jan Lutma, who though over twenty years older than Rembrandt died the same year, was the leading goldsmith in Amsterdam. His son was an etcher who may have been trained in Rembrandt's studio. One of the father's most celebrated commissions was the tulip beaker he made in 1652 for Nicolaas Tulp, whose anatomy lesson Rembrandt had painted at the very outset of his career in Amsterdam. The beaker was much prized by Tulp, and he left it to the Guild of Surgeons on his death. Lutma was portrayed with examples of his craft in his hand and beside him. 135

There was one discordant note in Rembrandt's dealings with his patrons in these years. A Portuguese Jewish merchant, Diego Andrada, complained that the portrait of a certain 'young girl' he had commissioned did not look like her. He had paid Rembrandt in advance. The balance was due on the completion of the picture. If Rembrandt was not prepared to make the portrait resemble the girl a little more closely, then he wanted his money back. The painter for his part was prepared to go no further without receiving the balance of payment, or at least security for it. When he had finished it he would put it before the officials of the Guild of St Luke for their opinion. If they sided with Andrada, he would change it. If Andrada did not like Rembrandt's proposed course of action, then the artist would finish the picture in his own time and sell it in an auction. Unfortunately neither the end nor the cause of the affair are known to us, though the incident shows Rembrandt's intransigence with patrons.

Although not without future strains, a happier relationship existed between Rembrandt and his Sicilian admirer from Messina. In 1652 Don Antonio Ruffo, whose large collection of pictures included three examples by the Utrecht artist Matthias Stomer, who had worked in Sicily, ordered a painting of a philosopher without further specification from Rembrandt, and was prepared to pay about eight times what an Italian artist would have received. Two years later Rembrandt delivered the painting of *Aristotle contemplating the Bust of Homer*. The patron was very pleased with the result, and shortly before ordering more pictures from the artist he asked Guercino to paint a pendant to it. He had chosen the right man. Guercino replied: 'As for the half figure of Rembrandt which has come into your hands, it cannot be other than complete perfection, because I have seen various works of his in prints which have come into our region. They are very beautiful in execution, engraved with good taste and done in a fine manner, so that one can assume that his work in colour is likewise complete exquisiteness and perfection. I sincerely esteem him as a great artist.' The tribute is so warm that it is all the sadder that today we can no longer see the result of Guercino's admiration put into practice, as the pendant is lost. And the next year Mattia Preti was also asked to paint a companion. In his letter to the Sicilian nobleman, he spoke of the 'two extremely beautiful works already in your possession', a remark which may of course amount to no more than a little flattery to please a patron.

What is unusual about Rembrandt's picture is that he was allowed to choose the subject, and for several years the patron remained uncertain of the correct identification. Guercino guessed that the subject was a physiognomist and painted a cosmographer as a companion. Although Rembrandt had painted a number of subjects from Classical mythology in the early 1630s, the *Aristotle* represents the first occasion on which he turned to one of the great figures of the Classical world. Moreover, his representation followed no recognizable pictorial tradition and was largely a compilation from varied sources unified by his own imagination. Regrettably it remains uncertain what if any deeper meaning the artist intended, although the general gist can easily be understood. Aristotle is shown with one hand on a bust of Homer, a poet whom he venerated, while around his neck he wears a gold chain of honour with a portrait medal probably of Alexander, to whom Aristotle had served as tutor. It may be added that Homer was much on Rembrandt's mind, since he was the subject of the drawing he made in Jan Six's *Album amicorum* in the

130

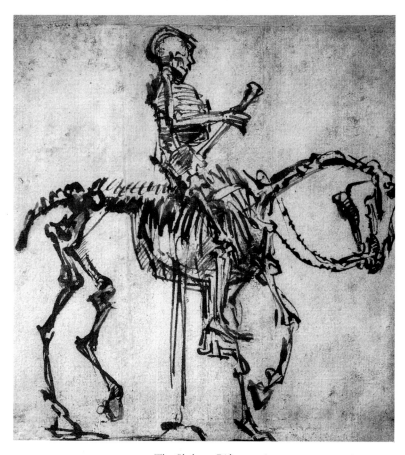

137 *The Skeleton Rider, c.* 1655

previous year. Moreover, Rembrandt owned busts of Aristotle and Homer, which were placed side by side in his 'gallery'. Whether or not the latter sparked Rembrandt's imagination, he used a standard Classical type for the bust of Homer, but when he came to treat Aristotle 'in the flesh' he chose as his model a bearded man, possibly a friend, who recurs unmistakably in another picture of this period (National Gallery). Aristotle's clothing, wide-brimmed hat, black apron and full sleeved gown, the last a recognizable studio prop, was largely fanciful and does not correspond in any way with Classical costume. The final result, quite unlike what the 'archaeological' approach of Rubens would have produced, is a work of mysterious authority and power. And as we shall see, it continued to mean something to Rembrandt, who later expanded on the theme of the three great men of the Classical world.

The first hint that Rembrandt was active again in the Anatomy Theatre
137  is given by his drawing of a skeleton rider. A German visitor to Amsterdam noted in his diary that he had seen in the Anatomy Theatre there 'a skeleton of a man on a skeleton of a horse', and this specimen must have served as Rembrandt's model. The sketch was probably made with no ulterior purpose, but later it came to hand when he was painting the *Polish Rider*.

Unlike the German visitor, Rembrandt's presence in the Anatomy Theatre was not due to idle curiosity. He was occupied on another major commission. The Anatomy Book records that 'On January 28 1656 there was punished with the rope Joris Fonteyn of Diest, who by the worshipful lords of the law court was granted to us as an anatomical specimen. On the 29th Dr Johan Deyman made his first demonstration on him in the theatre of the Anatomy, three lessons altogether.' It was probably this festive occasion that Rembrandt recorded for posterity in his second and last
136  *Anatomy Lesson*, which represents the dissection of the brain following the removal of the skull here seen in the hands of the surgeon's assistant. And this time we can be reasonably certain that an illustration to Vesalius' treatise provided the artist with the information he required for depicting the dissected part of the anatomy. Unfortunately fire destroyed the upper part of the picture in the eighteenth century and to see the whole
138  composition one has to resort to a drawing. This was probably made to show the design for the frame, rather than as a preparatory study, so the details are all too summarily sketched in.

By this time the Anatomy Theatre was in St Margaret's Hall, and it was
18  there that *The Anatomy Lesson of Dr Deyman* joined that of *Professor Tulp*.
19  Only at the end of the century did the surgeons return to the old weighhouse in the St Anthoniesmarkt, where a contemporary guide book to the city (1693) records the 'various paintings by unusually gifted artists, including two by the celebrated Rembrandt, which excel all the others'. Hung in the same room, the two paintings must have been a most eloquent lesson as to the changes that nearly a quarter of a century had wrought in Rembrandt's art. In *The Anatomy Lesson of Professor Tulp* we were at the theatre witnessing a performance. Nearly twenty-five years later the central figure is shown full face, with the body stretched out directly in front in strong foreshortening. He proceeds with all the majestic solemnity of the priest celebrating the Mass.

In his second anatomy lesson we are aware how Rembrandt arranges his composition in a much simpler pattern based primarily on horizontal and

164

138 *The Anatomy Lesson of Dr Johan Deyman, c.* 1656

vertical accents, using the architectural background as a carefully devised foil to articulate and monumentalize the subject before it. Space is limited but measured, and the figures are placed in the immediate foreground to powerful effect. Everything in the picture is reduced to essentials in a way calculated to involve the spectator almost subconsciously in the event taking place before his or her eyes. And to realize the new grandeur in his work of the 1650s, Rembrandt returned to a study of some of the great masters of the Italian High Renaissance, notably Leonardo, Raphael and Titian. It is ironic that at the same time a classical wave was influencing Dutch taste, but the results could not have been more different.

   *The Anatomy Lesson of Dr Deyman* was a work to which that stern critic of Rembrandt, Sir Joshua Reynolds, responded with unaccustomed warmth: 'There is something sublime in the character of the head, which reminds one of Michael Angelo; the whole is finely painted, the colouring much like Titian.' In the painting of the canvas, which Reynolds rightly

139 *St Jerome in an Italian Landscape, c.* 1653

140 *The Prophet Elisha with the Widow and her Sons, c. 1657*

admires, Rembrandt employed the enriched application of brushwork, described already in the portrait of *Jan Six*, but as always in these late works he varies his method to suit the subject in hand. In mentioning the name of Titian, Reynolds pointed to a major source of inspiration, visible in the free handling of the brush combined with the use of glazes, and the use of a rich but restricted palette. But in recognizing the older artist's achievement, Rembrandt maintains his own character, as a comparison of the different reds chosen by the two artists makes plain.

Hardly less important than colour was Rembrandt's new feeling for light and atmosphere, those twin obsessions of Venetian art. This is wonderfully apparent, whether he was producing a portrait such as that of *Dr Arnold Tholinx*, or representing figures in a landscape, as in the etching 132 of *St Jerome* and the drawing of *The Prophet Elisha with the Widow and her Sons*, in both of which the figures are suffused within the play of light covering the entire scene. And in the two religious works the links with Titian do not stop there, since the landscape setting is clearly Venetian in character, and represents a conscious change on Rembrandt's part from Dutch scenery. Moreover, in abandoning landscape as a subject on its own,

Rembrandt had sought to introduce a new scale of figure composition within a landscape setting. And in relating the latter, which served much the same function as architecture, to the figures, Rembrandt surely turned to Titian's example, which so memorably provides a measured setting harmonizing in mood with the human events taking place in the foreground.

Rembrandt's new concern for the effects of light was not limited to naturalistic representation. Whereas he had chosen subjects from Christ's childhood in the 1640s, he now became preoccupied with themes from the Passion, above all in his drawings and etchings. And in these he employed the consequence of light dissolving the forms of the figures to create a sense of mystery and awe. In the etching of *Christ appearing to the Apostles*, the radiance which shines forth from the diaphanous figure of Christ blinds his astonished companions, whereas in the drawing of *Christ taken Prisoner*, Christ towers above his pygmy-sized captors, who are transfixed like so many moths by the brilliance of light emanating from the figure of their victim. And in achieving this result, the artist once again displays his technical mastery. In the etching he devised a pattern of lightly bitten parallel lines, whereas an extensive application of wash in the drawing left

142

141 *Christ appearing to the Apostles*, 1656

142 *Christ taken Prisoner, c. 1656*

but little of the natural colour of the paper to provide the source of mystical light.

During the 1650s Rembrandt produced a series of Biblical drawings which should be regarded as works of art in their own right. They provided a means of expression of Rembrandt in private. There is little evidence whether they were sold, given to friends and patrons, or kept by the artist. A notable feature of the drawings is the way that in order to concentrate on the interpretation of the subject the degree of finish is kept to the minimum. In the imposing drawing of *Nathan admonishing David*, 143 we see no more than two summarily drawn figures in an abbreviated setting composed of curtain and column, intended as much to establish scale as to provide a recognizable ambiance. The fluid strokes of the reed pen are applied in a masterly way to suggest the interlocking of the two figures in their dialogue. In painting, etching and above all drawing, the history of David developed into a favourite theme, whether he was represented or referred to in absence, as in the painting of *Bathsheba*. In his 113 continuing predilection for two figures in dialogue or close relationship, Rembrandt no longer introduces a unifying motif such as a hand, but maintains the separate identities of each participant, thereby enhancing his

143 *Nathan admonishing David, c. 1655*

interpretation of the event. We become aware of two sides to the story, and in an inexplicable way of both past and future. Increasingly the artist came to concentrate on the essence of such themes as love, penitence and forgiveness, which become the fundamental subject instead of the incidents of the particular story in hand.

From 1650 onwards Rembrandt not only mastered a freedom of the techniques of painting, drawing and etching, which allowed him full expression of the subject in hand, but he also constantly varied both what he wanted to say and how he said it. It becomes increasingly difficult to offer meaningful generalizations about his work at a given period. As his imagination became more and more personal in its search for the basic meaning of a particular subject, so each work posed its own problems and required its own solutions. This situation may well be the cause of the number of unfinished pictures from later years left in the studio at the artist's death. It became ever more difficult to accept that the refinement he sought had finally been reached. But though many of his contemporaries may neither have understood nor admired what he did, there are relatively few failures in Rembrandt's last works.

## CHAPTER FIVE

# In adversity, immortality

Just as one tragic event took place in the year that Rembrandt finished one of his most important commissions, so in the year that he painted *The Anatomy Lesson of Dr Deyman* he had to face another personal catastrophe. It must have become increasingly clear to him that he was rapidly approaching bankruptcy.

Rembrandt had lost none of his natural extravagance. Baldinucci has a story that he was not only a lavish collector of other works of art but in order to stimulate the sales of his etchings 'at intolerable prices, he had them bought back all over Europe wherever he could find them, at any price'. Already five years after Saskia's death her family was very suspicious that Rembrandt was squandering Titus' inheritance. And there are records of a number of purchases of works of art at auctions during the 1640s to give substance to their concern. It was as a result of these anxious inquiries that Rembrandt had an assessment made of the value of their joint estate at the time of Saskia's death. This according to the artist amounted to 40,750 guilders. It is clear, however, from subsequent events that he had exaggerated and that the figure should have been about 30,000 guilders.

Real trouble did not start until 1653, the worst year of the general economic depression due to the reversals in the First Anglo-Dutch War, which led to near financial collapse in Amsterdam. In this year Rembrandt still owed just over half of the price of his house. He had paid no interest on the outstanding amount for the past five years, and in addition had allowed the legatees of the original owner, one of whom was Christoffel Thijsz, to pay the taxes on the house for the past three years.

Thijsz had been very tolerant but clearly felt that the time had come for the matter to be cleared up. On the other hand Rembrandt was not the full owner of the house, and in his high-handed way was not prepared to move in the matter until the deeds had been made out in his name. Thijsz agreed to arrange for this on the condition Rembrandt settled the outstanding payment. So in February 1653 Thijsz presented Rembrandt through a notary with the full account which amounted to 8,470 guilders with the interest included. At the same time Rembrandt borrowed two sums of 4,000 guilders, one from Isaac van Heertsbeeck and the other from Dr

Cornelis Witsen. The latter was a member of the Kloveniersdoelen, where the artist probably met him, and in this very year became Burgomaster of Amsterdam. He raised a third loan of 1,000 guilders from Jan Six, for which Rembrandt's long-suffering friend Lodewijk van Ludick, the merchant and art collector, stood as guarantor. It would appear that Rembrandt settled the outstanding payment on the house shortly afterwards. As far as his debts were concerned he was back where he started.

At the end of 1655 we learn that the artist intended to buy another house in the Handbooghstraat which belonged to Otto van Cattenborch, who was the brother of Dirck, the art dealer. Rembrandt sought to obtain a mortgage of 4,000 guilders and proposed to hand over paintings and etchings to the value of 3,000 guilders. One of the works specified was a portrait of Otto van Cattenborch to be etched from the life, and to be of the quality of Rembrandt's portrait etching of Jan Six. Van Ludick, and another close friend, Abraham Francen, acted as the artist's witnesses. About the same time he sold objects belonging to him – we no longer know what – at no less than seven public auctions held in December 1655 and on 1 January 1656, all of which took place at the Keizerskroon in the Calverstraat, the city's oldest inn which also served as auction rooms. Raising money by these means, Rembrandt may only have intended to improve his general financial position, but it is possible that he may have had Van Cattenborch's house specifically in mind. On the face of it Rembrandt might be accused of putting into practice Sickert's advice to a young painter who wants to get on: 'Take a large studio. If you cannot afford to take one, take two.' It seems more likely, however, that he was intending to move to a cheaper house, settling some of his debts with the balance, which would be all the greater since he was paying a little under half with works of art for the new house. For some unexplained reason the scheme came to nothing. The house was never bought, and the etching never made.

By May of the following year the situation had deteriorated. In a desperate gamble to save the house, which ultimately failed, Rembrandt appeared before the Court of Orphans and transferred the title of the house to Titus' name. He added that he remained responsible for all the debts. It was about this time that his family in Leiden was particularly stricken with poverty. One brother is described as 'notoriously poor', and his sister as 'half insolvent'.

In July his position was so precarious that the only course left open to him was to apply for a *cessio bonorum*, or legal cession of estate, a move only available to *bona fide* debtors. This measure avoided the stigma of

144 ANON. *The Keizerskroon Inn, Amsterdam*

bankruptcy and consequent imprisonment, and allowed the debtor considerable freedom. He had to declare all his assets and debts in full, and to explain why he had been forced into this position. Rembrandt gave the reason as 'losses suffered in business as well as damages and losses by sea', the latter suggesting that he speculated in overseas trade. It was up to the debtor to persuade the court of his good faith and honesty. The case was heard by a tribunal before which both the debtor and the creditors appeared (one of the Commissioners was Nicolaas Tulp's son). From what Rembrandt said in his petition, it is clear that he was as much the victim of the current economic situation as of his own extravagances.

Rembrandt's petition was granted, and on 25 and 26 July the Court of Insolvency, clearly with the artist's close co-operation, drew up an inventory of all Rembrandt's possessions in the house in the Breestraat. Although it must be remembered that a good number of works of art had

173

145 *Four Orientals under a Tree, c.* 1656

already been sold at the end of 1655, the 363 items give a fascinating *coup d'oeil* of the contents of the house. Apart from furniture and clothes, there were pistols, helmets, a death-mask of Frederick Henry, wind instruments, bamboo pipes, porcelain figures, oriental works of art, Venetian glass, and Classical statuary. All Rembrandt's own works in the house were included; over seventy paintings, hundreds of drawings, including 'A book bound in black leather with the best sketches of Rembrandt', and portfolios of etchings. There were 'three small dogs done from the life by Titus van Rijn'. His collection of paintings by other artists included examples by Seghers, Brouwer, Lievens, Lastman, Lucas van Leyden, Giorgione (owner's attribution!), Raphael, Palma Vecchio, Bassano. But the most extensive part of the collection was devoted to 'paper art'. The countless number of portfolios of drawings are surpassed in quantity only by those containing prints. The universality of his taste is shown by the contents. A sketchbook by Mantegna, drawings by Raphael, prints by Lucas van Leyden, Dürer, Barocci, Tempesta, Cranach, the Carracci, as well as by

146 *Abraham entertaining the Angels*, 1656

147 *Lot and his Daughters*, c. 1656

seventeenth-century Dutch artists. The few books included the Bible and a copy of Jan Six's tragedy *Medea*. This represented over twenty-five years' collecting and some dealing. (At least two items are described as being owned in half-share. It was a common practice for artists to augment their income by dealing.)

Among the items was a book of 'curious miniature drawings', which may have contained the originals of the copies Rembrandt made after Mogul miniatures about this time. He may have made his drawings out of affection for his soon to be sold miniatures. Some Mogul miniatures were certainly acquired by Maria Theresa from a Dutch source, and incorporated into the decoration of one of the rooms in Schloss Schönbrunn outside Vienna. Among these were some of the original compositions of Rembrandt's copies.

Specific as well as general reflections of the Mogul miniatures copied by Rembrandt occur in his work about this time. The arrangement of the four 145 elderly dervishes sipping tea, seated beneath a tree, is unmistakably recalled 146 in the grouping of Abraham supping with the angels in the etching of 1656 147 and Lot taking wine with his daughters in a drawing of the period. A more pervasive influence of the oriental physiognomy recorded in these miniatures occurs in a number of works, such as the face of David in the 143 drawing of *Nathan admonishing David*, or those of the two angels in the etching of Abraham just mentioned. Rembrandt in his search for authenticity may have come to consider these figures as representing the heirs of the people of the Old Testament in the same way he employed Jews as models for the New Testament. (Unlike other artists, Rembrandt portrays Christ as a Jew.)

From these and numerous other examples of other works of art, it is clear that Rembrandt made use of his collection as a treasure trove of motifs and ideas. But in addition to being an artistic investment, which also, as we have seen, played its part in teaching, the artist may have conceived his collection as having a purpose as an entity. The heterogeneous nature of his possessions seems to us a perfect embodiment of the width of his interests, but in fact both the arrangement and the contents, a combination of three basic categories, *Naturalia*, *Artificialia* and *Antiquitates*, correspond to the typical encyclopaedic collection of the sixteenth and seventeenth centuries. In building this type of collection, which differed from those of other contemporary artists, Rembrandt was consciously or unconsciously associating himself with the activities of the gentleman virtuoso. How seriously he would have regarded his collection as a status symbol remains an open question, although he might have had something of this in mind when he began buying works of art in the early 1630s.

148 *Self-portrait*, 1657

The law began to move at its usual snail-like pace. It took four years to settle the artist's affairs. It is not certain how long Rembrandt continued to live in the house in the Breestraat, but in 1658 a cupboard containing linen and Hendrickje's jewellery still stood in the hall. Rembrandt was allowed complete freedom of movement and to practise his art without hindrance, but he was only allowed to keep sufficient of his earnings to buy the necessities of life. He was in duty bound to hand over the remainder so that it could be put towards settling his debts. He probably continued to have pupils, since he was allowed to keep two stoves and several studio partitions from the sale of the house.

If outwardly the tenor of his life had changed little, the events were a painful blow to his independence and pride. That he was deeply hurt can be interpreted from the self-portrait painted in 1657, the worst year of his experiences. Matters had come to a head, but he was not yet free from the inquisition and publicity, nor did he know what the outcome would be. 'Mondo ladro, mondo rubaldo,' Rembrandt seems to mutter to himself. But if he was wounded he was not beaten. The mood is one of tragic resignation.

The first sale of the artist's possessions took place in September 1656, and the dispersal of his property continued in a series of sales up to the end of 1658. The house itself was sold in February of the latter year, but owing to the objections of various creditors the sale was not authorized for another twelve months. Even then pending various court actions the purchaser did not take possession until December 1660, and it was possibly only then that Rembrandt moved out. At the auction the house fetched 11,218 guilders, which, though nearly 2,000 guilders less than Rembrandt had paid, was a very good price considering the general economic depression. Rembrandt had chosen his house well.

149 Bill announcing the sale of Rembrandt's collection, 1658

DE Curateur over den Insol=
venten Boedel van Rembrant van Rijn / konstigh Schilder / sal / als by de E. E Heeren Commissari-
sen der Desolate Boedelen hier ter Stede daer toe ge-authorifeert / by Executie verkopen de voordere Papier Kunst onder den selven Boedel als noch berustende/ bestaende inde Konst van verscheyden der voornaemste so Italiaensche/ Fransche / Duytsche ende Nederlandtsche Meesters / ende by den selven Rembrant van Rijn met een groote curieusheyt te samen verfamelt.

Gelijck dan mede een goede partye van
Teeckeningen ende Schetsen vanden selven Rembrant van Rijn selven

De verkopinge sal wesen ten daeghe/
ure ende Jaere als boven / ten huyse van
Barent Jansz Schuurman / Waert in
de Keysers Kroon / inde Kalver straet/
daer de verkopinge voor desen is geweest,

Segget voort,

In September 1658 the collection of prints and drawings which had been kept apart from the rest of the artist's possessions was finally auctioned. A printed bill announced that a sale would take place at the Keizerskroon in 149 the Calverstraat of further 'paper art' consisting of examples by the most outstanding Italian, French, German and Netherlandish masters, and including a great part of the drawings and sketches made by Rembrandt himself. But the prices fetched were ridiculously low and the total proceeds amounted to just under 600 guilders.

The main legal battle revolved around Titus' dues. Rembrandt could no longer act as a trustee for his son and the court appointed an official to take over this job. Eventually the second holder of this post succeeded in establishing Titus as a preferential creditor. The immediate result of this decision was that one of Rembrandt's main creditors, Isaac van Heertsbeeck, had to hand back the money with which he had been repaid from the sale of the house. To be on the side of the angels is not to deny a certain sympathy to the unfortunate Van Heertsbeeck, who had lent the artist money to buy his house. At his death a few years later he included the loan among his hopeless debts.

The amount of Titus' claim was based on the valuation made in 1647, and one of the first legal inquiries was to establish how far it was accurate. It was in the interest of Rembrandt's creditors to prove that it was grossly exaggerated. Had they done so, Titus' putative share would have been reduced accordingly. Rembrandt for his part mustered a number of witnesses to support the accuracy of the valuation. Amongst these were two of the sitters in *The Night Watch* who testified as to the amount the artist was paid for the commission. Lodewijk van Ludick gave details about a painting by Rubens of *Hero and Leander* which Rembrandt had sold three years after Saskia's death. Hendrick van Ulenborch did the same for a portrait painted by Rembrandt in 1642. Rembrandt's fellow artist Philips Koninck described a pearl necklace he had bought from the artist seven years before. The silversmith Jan van Loo and his wife, whose daughter was to marry Titus, said that they had been on terms of great intimacy with the artist and his deceased wife. They proceeded to describe Saskia's jewellery, which included a diamond ring and a pair of earrings, pearls set in gold, bracelets of gold mail. The valuation was finally accepted as accurate, though this seeming smile of fortune froze very quickly. Titus' putative half of Saskia's estate was 10,000 guilders. In fact, it only amounted to 6,952 guilders, which was taken from the proceeds of the sale of the house.

By 1661 Rembrandt had satisfied the court over his legal obligations and he was free of all further restrictions. His creditors had either been paid – the burgomaster Witsen was the first to get his money back – or put in a position like Van Heertsbeeck in which they had little further legal redress against him. Some other debts had been amicably settled through the help of the artist's friends.

Jan Six had lent Rembrandt 1,000 guilders in 1653, though Lodewijk van Ludick had had to stand as guarantor. Six was either cautious or in need of the money, and two years later sold his bill to a merchant. When Rembrandt's financial crisis ensued the following year, the merchant made the unfortunate Van Ludick pay. An agreement was then made between the two friends, and Rembrandt was to pay the money back over three years with interest, and also include a painting, *David and Jonathan*, which 'he already has under hand'. Van Ludick had considerable difficulty in getting the money, though this was not entirely the artist's fault. Rembrandt appears never to have succeeded in delivering the painting. This was not the only such occasion, and apart from instances when there was a genuine disagreement between artist and patron as to what constituted finish, Rembrandt seems to have developed a reluctance to accept a work as complete. Houbraken records that he only considered 'a picture finished when the master had achieved his intentions', and presumably his intentions grew with each application of paint. Although it was his habit, mentioned by Baldinucci, to work on a number of pictures at the same time so as to allow each layer of paint to dry thoroughly, it is revealing that on his death he left a substantial number of incomplete pictures in his house. (The inventory lists four works as unfinished, as well as a group of twenty-two described as 'both finished and unfinished').

Rembrandt's other great friend of this time, who made a rather similar arrangement on his behalf, was Abraham Francen, the apothecary. He lived in the district to which the artist was to move. His house was situated in the Angelierstraat, which is farther on towards the River Y. They were already friends in 1653, when the artist gave him power of attorney, and apart from all he did for Rembrandt over his financial troubles, he acted as security for Titus at a later date, and finally became guardian to Rembrandt and Hendrickje's daughter, Cornelia. His last act for the Rembrandt family was to give Cornelia away in marriage.

150    In Rembrandt's portrait print, Francen, richly dressed, is seen among a collection of pictures and other works of art, which belie the modest means he is known to have possessed. It has been proposed that this plate was originally intended to portray Otto van Cattenborch, and when the sale of the house, referred to earlier, fell through, the features of the etched portrait included in the contract were changed to those of Francen. But, although much rework of the plate took place, it remains impossible to establish this. A vivid picture of Francen is provided by Gersaint, the first

150 *Abraham Francen, c. 1656*

cataloguer of the artist's etchings (1751): 'This Virtuoso had so strong a
Passion for Prints, that, as his Circumstances were narrow, he frequently
denied himself Victuals and Drink that he might be able to make a Purchase
that pleased him'.

In portraying his friend, whether he was the original sitter or not,
Rembrandt followed the same basic arrangement he had used for the
etched portrait of Six, placing the figure beside the window in the corner of
a room filled with possessions. But to ring the changes as he invariably did
in his etched portraits, he chose for the first and only time an oblong instead
of an upright format. This, it may not be coincidence, was the
transformation effected by Lorenzo Lotto to the upright High Renaissance
portrait of Titian. It allowed more of the room and its furnishings to be
included, which tell us as much about the character and interests as the face;
Francen like Six looks down absorbed by the paper he holds. The print also
offers a study in light as the sun floods through the window, illuminating
the sitter's face and catching the edges of the various objects in the room.

(The plate is also notable for the different states in which substantial changes were made to the original pose, so that in place of a straddled position across a stool, the sitter was comfortably ensconced in a high-backed armchair).

If the events of these years were extremely painful, not all those responsible for carrying out the orders of the court were unsympathetic towards the artist's plight. About the time that the dispersal of his property began, Rembrandt made a portrait, executed entirely in drypoint with some work with the burin, of Thomas Jacobsz. Haringh, warden of the Town Hall. One of his duties was the supervision of the auctioning of movable property in bankruptcy cases, and he was directly involved in several of the sales of the artist's possessions.

Rembrandt finally moved out of his grand house in the Breestraat and turned to a simpler dwelling on the other side of the city. This district, known as the Jordaan, had a character of its own quite unlike the rest of Amsterdam, and was largely inhabited by artisans and small shopkeepers. It is situated in an isolated position just beyond the Keizersgracht, the outermost of the three canals. Even today it stands apart, and still retains its

151 *Thomas Jacobsz. Haringh,*
*c.* 1656

152 ANON. *The Entrance Hall of the Artist's House on the Rozengracht*

atmosphere of peace and simple living. There Rembrandt lived in a house in the Rozengracht, which he rented for 225 guilders a year. Opposite the house there was a pleasure-garden decorated with statuary and fountains, known as the Labyrinth, which was run by the father of Johan Lingelbach, the painter. Rembrandt was not much over fifty when he moved here, but a hard life must have aged him prematurely. The peaceful and humble surroundings no doubt had a soothing effect. It was a district where no questions were asked. Everyone went their own way, totally absorbed in the struggle for existence.

153 *Titus, c. 1655*

During the last decade of his life, Rembrandt turned increasingly away from the outside world. He made no landscapes, only a few figure studies and fewer genre scenes. All was concentrated on the private world of his imagination. Here no material cares could affect him. We feel that the curtains have been drawn, and the outside scene shut out. Rembrandt has escaped into a timeless world.

Intense suffering often gives a sense of loneliness. If Rembrandt felt this keenly (and it is not difficult to imagine that for the artist as opposed to the man the second tragedy was worse than the first), he was not alone. The

154 *Hendrickje Stoffels* (detail), 1660

stalwart loving character of both Titus and Hendrickje came to the fore during these years, and they succoured him with their support and sympathy. Throughout all the events of the last decade of the artist's life, one is constantly aware of an indivisible trinity bound together by mutual love.

Although Rembrandt may have finished with the law, he now came up against the rules of his own guild, the Guild of St Luke, of which he had been a member since 1634. In the same year as the sale of his house and collection, the Guild introduced two new regulations which affected him acutely. These were aimed at booksellers and possibly art dealers, and not at artists, even if the effects were the same. The first regulation laid down that anyone selling up should do so immediately without any delay. The effect this probably had on the sale of Rembrandt's collection of prints and drawings has already been seen.

The second regulation was to affect his future. Any member who had sold up was in no circumstance allowed to carry on trade in the city, either in public or from his own house. In effect Rembrandt could no longer sell his works or deal in other works of art, even to earn the bare necessities of life.

It was then that Hendrickje and Titus rose to the occasion. Already in 1658, when Rembrandt's affairs were under consideration by the court, they had taken over the sale of his paintings and etchings, and had supervised the printing of the editions of his etchings. In order to get round the new edict of the Guild, they formed a company which would remain in force until six years after the artist's death. Rembrandt became their employee and handed over all his new works. He also acted as adviser for 'no one is more accomplished'. He received no salary, but was provided with free board and lodging. His immediate cares were looked after, and he could continue as a professional artist.

Rembrandt was not forgotten. He continued to have pupils up to his last years. The Dordrecht artist, Aert de Gelder, was last in a long line. He also proved to be among the most gifted, and whereas most of the other pupils turned to a more fashionable style, he continued to work in Rembrandt's manner into the eighteenth century.

Rembrandt also continued to receive a number of commissions in spite of his move out of the centre of the city. One unusual patron was Lieven Willemsz. van Coppenol, who formerly ran a school on the Singel. After a mental breakdown he took up calligraphy with an unbridled fanaticism, and at the same time commissioned several artists to etch or engrave his portrait, which he then sent to various poets to invite them for a fee to write a poem about him. In these years Rembrandt etched him twice. On some of the impressions the sitter has inscribed a poem in his flowing hand. The most intimate of the portraits of Coppenol is the etching showing him writing at his desk with his grandson Antonius looking over his shoulder. Above the desk are a pair of compasses and set squares. In a later stage of the etching Rembrandt added a triptych on the wall in place of the mysterious circle that was a feature of one of his greatest self-portraits.

No less than four poems were written in praise of Rembrandt's etchings of Coppenol. But as usual this popular literary exercise was more concerned with flattering the sitter than the artist. One of the four is

155

155 *Lieven Willemsz. van Coppenol with his Grandson, c.* 1658

addressed to Coppenol the 'Phoenix calligrapher', not to Rembrandt the 'Phoenix artist'.

Another unusual commission was the result of a chance encounter in the street in 1665 between Titus and a Leiden bookseller, who asked the former whether he knew an engraver. When Titus recommended his father, the bookseller said: 'I have heard that your father etches but not cuts; this little plate has to be cut.' Persuaded by Titus that 'my father cuts as curiously as anyone', the bookseller commissioned a portrait of the recently deceased Leiden professor of medicine, Jan Antonides van der Linden, which was to serve as the frontispiece to his edition of Hippocrates. In the event Rembrandt, who had to take his likeness from a portrait by Van den Tempel, produced a mixture of etching, drypoint and burin unsuitable for mass reproduction, and hence it was never used.

156 *Gerard de Lairesse*, 1665

In the same year, Gérard de Lairesse, a precocious young painter from Liège, arrived in Amsterdam and was painted by Rembrandt. Perhaps the informality of the pose suggests a friendly commission from a fellow-artist. In colour it is a sombre work composed primarily of black and white, with only the golden curls providing variation. The effects of syphilis, from which De Lairesse suffered, are skilfully mitigated by Rembrandt. The very broad execution seen a decade earlier in the portrait of Jan Six is here used consistently throughout and gives the picture an imposing unity.

De Lairesse at first admired Rembrandt and worked in his manner, but he changed to the prevailing classicizing style. Towards the end of the century he went blind and took to writing about art theory. At the time he wrote it was hardly surprising that Rembrandt's art became an example of what not to do. To a strict application of classical rules, he added the then not uncommon criterion of judging a painter by the social status of his sitters. 'Rubens and Van Dyck, who were daily at court and who spent their time with nobles, established their thoughts on the heights of art;

157 *Jeremias de Decker*, 1666

Jordaens and Rembrandt on the other hand, are *bourgeois*', and so on. Fortunately, Rembrandt was not alive to hear such criticism, which was to dog his reputation throughout the eighteenth century.

If Vondel manifested little enthusiasm for Rembrandt, his pupil Jeremias de Decker, a hardly less famous poet, had no hesitation in describing himself as a friend of the artist, and he merited this title by the number of flattering references he made to Rembrandt's work in his poems. He particularly admired the artist's ability to translate a Biblical text into the medium of paint and to 'bring the dead so well to life'. Rembrandt painted at least two portraits of him, though only one exists today. In gratitude De Decker wrote a poem addressed to Rembrandt; Alexander the Great only allowed himself to be painted by Apelles, and though the poet does not share the former's pride he is nevertheless flattered to be painted by the Apelles of his day. Rembrandt's work even surpasses that of Raphael and Michelangelo. What more could a classicist Dutchman say?

Living out on the Rozengracht, Rembrandt was not in fact forgotten by

158 GOVAERT FLINCK *The Conspiracy of Julius Civilis, c.* 1659

the men who ran the city. He was still at the back of their minds as a useful
painter to be summoned in an emergency. In 1655 they inaugurated the
new Town Hall, but the lunettes in the large gallery surrounding the main
hall still had to be decorated with eight paintings. A suitable subject was
chosen; the revolt of the Batavians under their leader Julius Civilis against
the Romans, as described by Tacitus. The subject had particular
significance for the Dutch people, who regarded the Batavians as their
forerunners, and more specifically the struggle for freedom from the
Romans as the prototype for the War of Independence against Spain,
which had only recently been finally settled in Holland's favour at the
Treaty of Munster. This choice commission went to Rembrandt's
erstwhile pupil Govaert Flinck, but no sooner had he prepared the sketches

159 *The Conspiracy of Julius Civilis, c. 1661*

than he died. The city fathers had to think again, and in a spirit of compromise they commissioned Lievens, Jordaens and Rembrandt to produce one painting each. (Rembrandt's former cousin by marriage, Hendrick van Ulenborch, had already been employed on cleaning and varnishing paintings in the Town Hall.)

Rembrandt was given the first scene, depicting the banquet given by Julius Civilis to his fellow-conspirators, under cover of which they swear their complicity in ousting the Romans. He finished the painting and in 1662 it was *in situ* in the Town Hall. The following year, however, it had been removed and replaced by the work of a very inferior artist, Jurriaen Ovens, who did no more than work up Flinck's original *modello*. Rembrandt's painting was greatly cut down, presumably by the artist to

163

make it more saleable, and its appearance can only be glimpsed in a drawing. We do not know the reason for this débâcle; since the work was praised in a poem (those touchstones of popular taste) it seems more likely that its removal was due to a conflict between the intransigent painter and the city fathers, rather than public criticism of the painting itself. One possible source of disagreement may have been Rembrandt's interpretation of the subject. Flinck in his preparatory drawing for this scene represents the oath-taking in the Roman manner of clasping right hands, a mode which would have matched the classical spirit of the building. Rembrandt, a more accurate interpreter of history, follows Tacitus by depicting the ceremony of taking the oath according to *barbaro ritu*, in which the ends of the swords are placed together. Moreover, by placing Julius Civilis in profile, Flinck neatly avoids the disturbing fact that, according to Tacitus, the Batavian leader only had one eye, a feature awesomely revealed in Rembrandt's picture. Given the association of identity between the Batavians and the Dutch, the city fathers may have considered a gain in historical accuracy was more than outweighed by a lack of classical decorum. Indeed one would hardly wish to identify one's spiritual ancestors among the ruffianly conspirators gathered together at that strange barbaric rite. Moreover, Rembrandt executed the canvas in the most summary fashion, applying paint with the palette knife in broad areas of colour, to produce a style very different from that of the other contributors. This might well have been found unacceptable by patrons more used to the current vogue for a smooth finish. Whatever the cause of the dispute it must have confirmed Rembrandt in his feelings about the new Town Hall and all those within it.

The original work, which measured some 19 feet (5.8 metres) in both directions, depended greatly, as can be seen in the preliminary drawing, on the massive architecture. In reducing the work to more saleable proportions the artist kept the central scene with the conspirators arranged around the table in a manner which once again in Rembrandt's work presents a variation on Leonardo's *Last Supper*. By reducing the size of the canvas Rembrandt has increased the impact of the scene of oath-taking. A source of light from within the picture, hidden from the spectator, illumines the figures huddled together and creates a strongly eerie atmosphere. For once, chiaroscuro is kept subordinate to colour, which though limited in range, primarily yellow, brown and red, glows in the nocturnal scene. Although the distant position of the picture's original destination may have been a determining factor, we cannot but feel that its primitive manner of execution was deliberately employed to match the character of the event it portrayed.

160 *The Portrait of the Syndics of the Clothmakers' Guild*, 1662

Rembrandt had far happier relations with another city institution, the Clothmakers' Guild, for whom he completed a group portrait in 1662. The picture was to hang in their hall, the Staalhof, in the Staalstraat, just round the corner from the Nieuwe Doelenstraat, where Rembrandt had spent a happy period with Saskia. The five men with their servant in the background were the comptrollers of the cloth samples, who were elected annually and met in private in the Staalhof. The book to which their chairman points so categorically can be identified as the sample book which provided the standard against which the cloth was tested. Unlike the usual statically posed group portrait, Rembrandt has enlivened and unified his portrayal by depicting an imaginary moment in their discussion. Although there was no audience to witness the deliberations, Rembrandt has made the spectator the focus of attention of the five governors, who intently look in his direction from their various positions around the heavily foreshortened table. The low viewpoint, which heightens the spectator's sense of bowing to authority, may have been dictated by the picture's original position above a fireplace.

161 *Homer dictating to a Scribe, c.* 1663

But the work can be read as more than a highly realistic portrayal of a committee meeting in action. The inclusion of a beacon, seen in an inserted panel in the right background, was accepted in the general sense as a symbol of good citizenship and government. The five men who maintain the standards on the basis of their sample book were devised as an exemplar of good administration to influence future holders of the office.

The powerful simplicity of the picture belies the effort which went into creating the work. X-rays disclose that the artist made a number of important changes in the positions of several figures in the course of execution. Specifically the figure of the servant, a minor person in the portrait but an essential pivot in the composition, was tried out in different positions. The exact placement of each figure was crucial to the final result, and the artist's improvisation reveals how he worked directly on the canvas, whether he had some working drawings, as on this occasion, or not. And in establishing the final arrangement, he relied on the horizontal

162 *Homer*, 1663

and vertical lines of the heavy panelling, so evocative of the stuffy atmosphere of the room, to play an essential supporting role to the figures. Once again the colour harmony of red, brown and black is simple but striking.

Rembrandt's Sicilian admirer Ruffo still provided some comfort to the painter in his last years. In 1661 he ordered two more pictures, which we learn from a shipping bill were *Alexander the Great* and a *Homer*. In providing two more pictures to hang with the *Aristotle*, Rembrandt extracted the two subsidiary figures from the latter and made them into

130

163 *The Conspiracy of*
*Julius Civilis*, 1661

subjects on their own. The *Homer* was subsequently damaged by fire and    162
cut down, but some idea of its original appearance can be gained from a
preliminary study, which includes the figure of the scribe assisting the blind    161
poet. (A change must have been made on the canvas since a later inventory
describes Homer as 'giving instruction to two disciples'.) Ruffo's
commission did not, however, pass off entirely smoothly. The patron
complained that the artist had made the half-figure of Alexander merely by
enlarging an existing canvas of a study of a head. The Dutch consul in
Messina, who became involved as an intermediary, reported that the

picture was 'painted on four pieces of cloth sewn together, whereby such ugly seams have resulted that it is incredible. . . . In Ruffo's entire collection, which consists of 200 pieces of the best masters in Europe, there is no other painting put together like this one out of pieces of cloth'. In addition Rembrandt was slow in producing the *Homer* and when it finally reached Ruffo he sent it back as 'but half finished and of such a nature that he should do as much again to it in order to make it come up to standard'. Rembrandt for once must have obliged. It would seem that Ruffo took these difficulties in his stride and they did nothing to lessen his admiration. In the very year of Rembrandt's death he ordered and received 189 of the master's etchings.

In 1667 Rembrandt was still a figure to be reckoned with in the city of Amsterdam. When Cosimo de Medici, later Grand Duke of Tuscany, visited Amsterdam, he went to see the artist. Apparently Rembrandt had nothing finished in his studio to show him and he was taken to other collections to find suitable works. Unfortunately the diary of Cosimo's companion is anything but informative about the visit. He only expands when discussing the weather, where he shows the typical preoccupation with fog of every Italian traveller in the North. But Cosimo probably returned to Florence with the self-portrait which formed part of his collection. By this time these attentions can have meant little to Rembrandt. He was terribly short of money. He sold Saskia's grave in the Oude Kerk. No price is mentioned, but this can hardly have alleviated the poverty, since he is unlikely to have got more than 200 guilders. He turned to Harman Becker, who was a dealer in jewels, textiles and other merchandise. He was also a keen collector, who eventually owned either fourteen or sixteen paintings by Rembrandt. He was in the habit of lending money to artists, provided they offered some of their works as pledges. In 1662 and 1663 Rembrandt twice borrowed sums of money from Becker on generous terms, and handed over nine paintings and two sketchbooks or albums. Two years later he was able to redeem his pledges, but by this time Becker had bought the bill for that original loan from Six from Lodewijk van Ludick, who had by now despaired seeing the return of his 1,000 guilders. Becker showed himself a firm creditor, and he was not averse to a little exploitation. On one occasion he insisted on Rembrandt finishing the painting *Juno* before he would allow the artist to settle his debts with him. Nevertheless it is fair to add that Becker was a realist and unlike the unfortunate Van Ludick he eventually got his picture, although whether he was satisfied with its 'finish', history does not relate.

It is perhaps legitimate to read something of Rembrandt's feelings in his self-portrait in the guise of St Paul, which may well have formed part of a series of apostles and evangelists he was working on at the time. It is highly

164

198

164 *Self-portrait as St Paul*, 1661

165 *The Jewish Bride, c.* 1668

significant that Rembrandt chose to portray himself in the role of that militant and undaunted apostle. But already he strikes us an actor in one of his greatest roles, for which he has grown too old.

The art-dealing partnership between Titus and Hendrickje was of short duration. On Sunday 7 August 1661, Hendrickje appeared before the notary to make her will. He described her as 'sick in appearance though still on her feet and active', a condition already to be observed in the moving portrait of her in the previous year. The intimate relationship she had with Rembrandt and Titus is shown by her wish that if Cornelia died childless Titus would become her heir. She struggled on for another two years and before she finally succumbed she had the satisfaction of being described as Rembrandt's wife. They were probably never married, but one hopes she was still able to appreciate the courtesy title. It went some way towards compensating for the reference to her as 'Rembrandt's concubine' in

154

Clement de Jonghe's list of the master's etchings. She was less than forty years old at her death in July 1663, possibly from the plague, which became an epidemic in Amsterdam in this year and was particularly prevalent in the poor district of the Jordaan. She was buried in the Westerkerk only a few minutes' walk from where they lived. Two days later Rembrandt acted as a witness for his landlord, whose son had also just died in the house on the Rozengracht.

Titus took over the art firm on Hendrickje's death, and continued to look after his father's affairs. There is a record of the father giving his son power of attorney. Titus was also an artist, trained, as one might suspect, by his father. In the inventory of the house in the Breestraat several paintings by Titus were mentioned. There are as well a number of signed drawings. *Meleager and Atalanta* rightly pays homage in style, if not in subject-matter, 167 to the person in whose cause he so valiantly fought.

166 Rembrandt's and Titus's signatures on a document dated 3 June 1665

In 1665, when he was twenty-four, Titus, supported by his father and their friend Abraham Francen, the art-dealer, appealed to the States General to allow him to come of age, since his business affairs were much hampered by his being a minor. This request was finally granted and he was paid his share of 6,952 guilders from the sale of the house in the Breestraat which had been held in trust for him. No sooner had this problem been solved than a fresh one arose. The following year their landlord died and their house was put up for auction. Fortunately the new owner allowed them to remain.

In February 1668 Titus married Magdalena van Loo, daughter of the silversmith, Jan van Loo. The parents were very old friends of Rembrandt's and had testified on his behalf when the valuation on his property made in 1647 was put in doubt at the time of his insolvency. Magdalena lived with her mother in a house on the Singel, opposite the Apple Market, where after their marriage Titus went to join them. The artist was left alone with his daughter Cornelia who was now fourteen years old.

Rembrandt must about this time have painted the work generally known as the *Jewish Bride*. Numerous attempts have been made to identify

167 TITUS VAN RIJN *Meleager and Atalanta*

the subject of the picture. Does it represent Isaac and Rebecca or Jacob and Rachel or one of several other possible Biblical couples? Or is it a portrait of Titus and his bride, the least convincing explanation, or of the Jewish poet, Miguel de Barrios and his wife? Or following the fashion of the time, is it a Biblical scene in which one of the couples is acting the roles? The couple, originally seated as X-rays show, stand side by side. He appears to have placed a gold chain around her neck and his right hand remains on her breast, a gesture she reciprocates in acquiescence by placing her hand on his. She may hold a piece of fruit in the other hand. It is work of utmost simplicity and represents one of the greatest expressions of the tender fusion of spiritual and physical love in the history of painting. Probably more tellingly than any other work, it demonstrates Rembrandt's capacity to isolate the essence of a story and immortalize it devoid of the specific

168 *Self-portrait*, 1669

connotations of a particular story. (If the picture represents Isaac and Rebecca, it is significant that Rembrandt omits the figure of Abimelech spying upon the couple included in a drawing of this subject probably executed a little earlier.)

The intimacy and poetry of the scene is conveyed by the warmth of colours harmonized beneath the softly glowing light which plays over the two figures. His golden sleeve is contrasted with the ample expanse of red of her dress, with her sleeves echoing the colour of his tunic. The background architecture and landscape are a neutral green and brown. The paint applied layer upon layer with both the brush and palette knife miraculously suggests the depth of feeling inherent in the picture.

Although it is unlikely that the picture had any direct association with Titus and Magdalena, it surely reflects the emotions that the newly married couple must have felt. Their happiness lasted no more than seven months. By September Titus was dead. He was buried in the Westerkerk. Six months later Magdalena gave birth to a daughter who was named Titia, in memory of her father.

Two self-portraits very different in mood show Rembrandt in the year of his death. In one if he does not appear actually senile, at least he has the air
168 of having reached a stage where nothing could touch him. In the other there is more than a touch of his habitual independence and determination as he clasps his hands with a sardonic expression on his face. X-rays reveal that he originally depicted himself with brush and maulstick in hand, but subsequently removed these symbols of his profession. By this time he had suffered every loss he could with the exception of his fifteen-year-old daughter, who no doubt tried to do everything she could to alleviate his sorrows. Her lot was hardly happy, and not helped by their extreme poverty. Magdalena complained bitterly that Rembrandt was dipping into her daughter's share of the estate in order to keep the house. Houbraken, writing of Rembrandt's simple tastes, says he was content to make a meal out of bread and cheese or a pickled herring. The Dutch writer makes a virtue out of necessity. Finally on 4 October 1669 he died. Four days later
169 his body went to join those of Hendrickje and Titus in the Westerkerk. His death went unnoticed by the outside world.

The day after the artist's death an inventory of his possessions was drawn up. The company formed by Hendrickje and Titus was still in existence and Magdalena was anxious to establish the claims of her daughter against those of Cornelia. Instead of the 363 items of various works of art and *objets d'art* listed in 1656, the list consisted of fifty items mainly of furniture and other household effects, as well as the pictures already mentioned. But on the orders of Magdalena van Loo, the remaining property consisting of

De Wester Kerck begonnen A°. 1620, de eerste Predicatie daer in gedaen op Pinxterdach 1631.

169 F. DE WIT *The Westerkerk, Amsterdam*

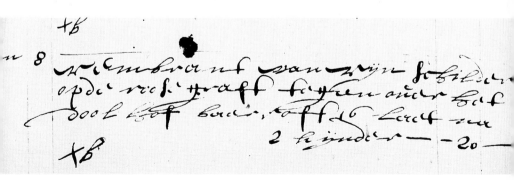

170 Notice of Rembrandt's Burial

paintings, drawings, 'rarities' and antiquities were locked away in three rooms. What these consisted of remains largely unknown, although two days before the artist died an amateur genealogist visited him and made notes about 'Antiquities and Rarities collected over a course of time by Rembrandt van Rijn'. The items mentioned are mainly pieces of armour, although there are also 'four flayed arms and legs anatomized by Vesalius', all of which suggest that even after his financial débâcle he continued to collect the kind of object which had taken his fancy from his earliest days.

The remainder of the story of Rembrandt's descendants is soon told. His daughter-in-law died six weeks after him, and was also buried in the Westerkerk. Among her possessions were a number of works of art, including 'three albums of priceless prints made by Rembrandt van Rijn during his life', as well as portraits of Rembrandt, Saskia and Titus, which were only listed among the furniture. The two orphans, Cornelia and Titia, were the only ones left. Their guardians, Abraham Francen for Cornelia, and Frans van Bylert for Titia, were involved in a long legal debate over the division of the estate, since by law Cornelia was illegitimate.

In later years Titia married the son of her guardian and died only in 1725 as the last member of the artist's family. The year after Rembrandt's death Francen gave Cornelia away in marriage to a painter, Cornelis Suythof. They left almost immediately for Batavia, where Cornelia gave birth to two children. With true filial piety, she christened them Rembrandt and Hendrickje.

For posterity Rembrandt left a substantial body of paintings, drawings and etchings, whose warm humanity, psychological insight and comprehensive variety offer some of the most absorbing, moving and elevating works in the history of art. Although created at one time in one place they possess a timeless universal validity.

# List of illustrations

*Measurements are given in inches followed by centimetres, height preceding width*

References:

Br.  A. Bredius (ed. H. Gerson), *The Paintings of Rembrandt*, 2nd ed., London 1969

B.  Bartsch – see C. White and K. Boon, *Rembrandt's Etchings*, Amsterdam, 1969

Ben.  O. Benesch, *Rembrandt's Drawings*, 2nd. ed., London, 1973

1 Notice of Rembrandt's registration as a student, 1620. Leiden University

2 Pieter Bast, *View of Leiden* (detail), 1601. Engraving. 7 × 18 (18.2 × 45). British Museum, London

3 Pieter Bast, *Bird's eye view of Leiden* (detail), 1600. Engraving. 15 × 16 (37.5 × 44). Leiden University

4 Rembrandt, *The Artist's Father(?)*, c. 1630. Red and black chalk with brown wash. 7 × 9 (18.9 × 24). Ben. 56. Ashmolean Museum, Oxford

5 Rembrandt, *Old Woman: the Artist's Mother(?)*, c. 1629. Panel. 20 × 14 (50 × 35). Br. 70. Windsor Castle. Reproduced by gracious permission of Her Majesty the Queen

6 Pieter Lastman (1583–1633), *The Angel and the Prophet Balaam*, 1622. Panel. 19 × 24 (48.5 × 61). Richard L. Feigen & Co., New York

7 Jan Lievens (1607–1674), *Self-portrait*, c. 1635. Panel. 16⁹⁄₁₆ × 13 (42 × 33). Present whereabouts unknown. Photo courtesy Noortman & Brod, London

8 Rembrandt, *Self-portrait Bareheaded*, 1629. Etching. 7 × 6 (17.8 × 15.4) B. 338. British Museum, London

9 Rembrandt, *Self-portrait*, c. 1631. Panel. 14¾ × 11⁷⁄₁₆ (37.5 × 29). Br. 6. Mauritshuis, The Hague

10 Jan Lievens (1607–1674), *Portrait of Rembrandt*, c. 1628. Panel. 22⁷⁄₁₆ × 17⅝ (57 × 44.7). Rijksmuseum, Amsterdam, on loan from Daan Cevat

11 Jan Lievens (1607–1674), *Constantijn Huygens* (detail), 1626–7. Panel. 39 × 33 (99 × 84). Douai Museum. Photo Rijksmuseum, Amsterdam

12 Rembrandt, *The Angel and the Prophet Balaam*, 1626. Panel. 25 × 18 (65 × 47). Br. 487. Musée Cognacq Jay, Paris. Photo Bulloz

13 Rembrandt, *Judas returning the Thirty Pieces of Silver*, 1629. Panel. 31 × 40 (79.5 × 102). Private Collection

14 Rembrandt, *The Presentation in the Temple*, 1631. Panel. 24¾ × 18⅞ (61 × 48). Br. 543. Mauritshuis, The Hague

15 Cornelis Danckerts, *Map of Amsterdam*, 1654. Engraving. Leiden University (Bodel Nijenhuis Collection). Photo Leiden University

16 Reinier Nooms, called Zeeman, *The Rokin with the Exchange in the Background, Amsterdam*. Etching. 5 × 9 (13 × 23.1). British Museum, London

17 Thomas de Keyser (1596/7–1667), *The Anatomy Lesson of Dr Sebastian Egbertsz*, 1619. Canvas 53⅛ × 73¼ (135 × 186). Historisch Museum, Amsterdam

18 Rembrandt, *The Anatomy Lesson of Professor Tulp*, 1632. 65 × 86 (162.5 × 216.5). Br. 403. Mauritshuis, The Hague

19 Reinier Nooms, called Zeeman, *The Anthoniesmarkt, Amsterdam*. Etching. 5 × 10 (13.5 × 24.7). British Museum, London

20 Rembrandt, *A Bearded Old Man*, 1634. Pen and brown wash. 3½ × 3 (8.9 × 7.1). Ben. 257. Royal Library, The Hague

21 Rembrandt, *Saskia in a Straw Hat*, 1633. Silverpoint on vellum. 7 × 4 (18.5 × 10.7). Ben. 427. Kupferstichkabinett, Staatliche Museen zu Berlin

22 Rembrandt, *Jan Cornelis Sylvius*, 1634. Etching. 7 × 5 (16.7 × 14). B. 266, i. British Museum, London

23 Rembrandt, *Saskia Asleep in Bed*, c. 1635. Pen and brush and brown ink. 5 × 8 (13.7 × 20.3). Ben. add. 4. Ashmolean Museum, Oxford

24 Rembrandt, *Saskia as Flora*, 1634. Canvas. 49 × 40 (125 × 101). Br. 102. Hermitage, Leningrad

25 Rembrandt, *Self-portrait with Saskia*, c. 1635. Canvas. 63 × 52 (161 × 131). Br. 30. Gemäldegalerie Alte Meister, Staatliche Kunstsammlungen, Dresden

26 Rembrandt, *Self-portrait with Saskia*, 1636. Etching. 5 × $3\frac{3}{4}$ (10.4 × 9.5). B. 19, i. British Museum, London

27 Rembrandt, *Saskia with One of her Children*, *c.* 1637. Red chalk. 5 × 4 (14.1 × 10.6). Ben. 280a. Courtauld Institute Galleries, London (The Princes Gate Collection)

28 R. Vinckeles, *The Doelenstraat, Amsterdam.* Drawing. Municipal Archives, Amsterdam

29 Rembrandt, *The Shipbuilder and his Wife* (Jan Rijcksen and Griet Jans), 1633. Canvas. $45\frac{1}{4}$ × 65 (115 × 165). Br. 408. Reproduced by gracious permission of Her Majesty the Queen

30 Thomas de Keyser (1596/7–1667), *Constantijn Huygens with his Clerk(?)*, 1627. Panel. $36\frac{3}{8}$ × $27\frac{5}{16}$ (92.4 × 69.3). National Gallery, London

31 Rembrandt, *Marten Soolmans*, 1634. Canvas. 82 × 53 (209 × 134). Br. 199. Private Collection. Photo Rijksmuseum, Amsterdam

32 Rembrandt, *Oepjen Coppit*, 1634. Canvas. 82 × 53 (209 × 134). Br. 342. Private Collection. Photo Rijksmuseum, Amsterdam

33 Rembrandt, *Jan Uytenbogaert, the Preacher*, 1635. Etching, touched with black chalk. 10 × 7 (25 × 18.7). B. 279. British Museum, London

34 Rembrandt, *Samuel Menasseh ben Israel*, 1636. Etching. 6 × 4 (14.9 × 10.7) B. 269, i. British Museum, London

35 Rembrandt, *Cornelis Claesz. Anslo*, 1640. Red chalk, pen and brown and grey wash, heightened with white. 10 × 8 (24.6 × 20.1). Ben. 759. Louvre, Paris (Rothschild Bequest)

36 Rembrandt, *Herman Doomer*, 1640. 29 × 21 (73 × 54). Br. 217. The Metropolitan Museum of Art, New York. (Bequest of Mrs H. O. Havemeyer, 1929. The H. O. Havemeyer Collection)

37 P. Pontius, *Frederick Henry, Prince of Orange* (detail), 1628. Engraving after the painting by Van Dyck. 19 × 14 (49.3 × 34.9). British Museum, London

38 Rembrandt, *Amalia van Solms*, 1632. Canvas. 27 × 29 (68.5 × 55.5). Br. 99. Musée Jacquemart André, Paris. Photo Bulloz

39 Rembrandt's second letter to Constantijn Huygens, 1636. 10 × 7 (25.5 × 18). British Museum, London

40 Rembrandt, *The Descent from the Cross*, 1633. Panel. 37 × 27 (93 × 68). Br. 550. Alte Pinakothek, Munich

41 Rembrandt, *The Resurrection*, 1639. Canvas. 37 × 27 (93 × 69). Br. 561. Alte Pinakothek, Munich

42 Rembrandt, *Jan Uytenbogaert, the Receiver-General*, 1639. Etching. 10 × 8 (25 × 20.4). B. 281, ii. British Museum, London

43 Rembrandt, *The Blinding of Samson*, 1636. Canvas. 94 × 113 (238 × 287). Br. 501. Städelsches Kunstinstitut, Frankfurt am Main

44 Anon. 16th-century Milanese artist, *The Last Supper, after Leonardo da Vinci.* Engraving. 9 × 18 (23 × 45). British Museum, London

45 Rembrandt, *The Last Supper, after Leonardo da Vinci*, *c.* 1635. Red chalk. 14 × 19 (36.5 × 47.5). Ben. 443. Metropolitan Museum of Art, New York, Robert Lehman Collection

46 Rembrandt, *Samson's Wedding Feast*, 1638. Canvas. $49\frac{3}{16}$ × $69\frac{1}{8}$ (126.5 × 175.5). Br. 507. Gemäldegalerie Alte Meister, Staatliche Kunstsammlungen, Dresden. Photo Gerhard Reinhold, Leipzig-Mölkau

47 Rembrandt, *Calvary*, *c.* 1635. Pen and brown ink, heightened with white. $8\frac{9}{16}$ × $7\frac{1}{16}$ (21.8 × 17.9). Ben. 108. Kupferstichkabinett, Staatliche Museen zu Berlin

48 Rembrandt, *The Annunciation to the Shepherds*, 1634. Etching and drypoint. $10\frac{5}{16}$ × $8\frac{9}{16}$ (26.2 × 21.8). B. 44, iii. British Museum, London

49 Rembrandt, *The Death of the Virgin*, 1639. Etching and drypoint. $16\frac{3}{8}$ × $12\frac{3}{8}$ (40.9 × 31.5). B. 99, ii. British Museum, London

50 Rembrandt, *The Preaching of St John the Baptist* (detail), *c.* 1636. Canvas on panel. $24\frac{7}{16}$ × $31\frac{1}{2}$ (62 × 80). Br. 555. Gemäldegalerie, Staatliche Museen zu Berlin

51 Rembrandt, *Woman with a Child frightened by a Dog*, *c.* 1635. Pen and brown ink. $4\frac{1}{8}$ × 4 (10.5 × 10.1). Ben. 403 *recto.* Fondation Custodia (Collection F. Lugt), Institut Néerlandais, Paris

52 Rembrandt, *Beggar warming his Hands*, *c.* 1630. Etching. $3\frac{1}{16}$ × $1\frac{13}{16}$ (7.7 × 4.6). B. 173, ii. British Museum, London

53 Rembrandt, *Jew Praying*, *c.* 1634. Pen and brown ink. $3\frac{7}{16}$ × $4\frac{3}{8}$ (8.8 × 11.1). Ben. 245. Staatliche Graphische Sammlung, Munich

54 Rembrandt, *Two Butchers at Work*, *c.* 1635. Pen and brown ink. $5\frac{7}{8}$ × $7\frac{7}{8}$ (14.9 × 20). Ben. 400. Städelsches Kunstinstitut, Frankfurt am Main

55 Rembrandt, *The Pancake Woman*, 1635. Etching. $4\frac{3}{16}$ × $3\frac{1}{16}$ (10.7 × 7.7). B. 124, ii. British Museum, London

56 Rembrandt, *A Negro Commander and Kettle-Drummer on Horseback*, *c.* 1638. Pen and brown wash, red chalk, yellow watercolour and white body-colour. 8 × 6 (20.9 × 16.3). Ben. 365. British Museum, London

57 Rembrandt, *Elephant*, *c.* 1637. Black chalk. 7 × 10 (17.8 × 25.6). British Museum, London

58 Rembrandt, *A Scene from Vondel's 'Gijsbrecht van Amstel'*, *c.* 1638. Pen and brown ink with white body-colour. $8\frac{1}{4}$ × $6\frac{1}{2}$ (20.9 × 16.5). Ben. 122.

Herzog Anton Ulrich-Museum, Brunswick
59 Rembrandt, *Swimmers*, 1651. Etching. $4\frac{3}{16}$ × $5\frac{3}{8}$ (11 × 13.7) B. 195, i. British Museum, London
60 Rembrandt, *A Woman on the Gallows*, 1664. Pen and ink with brown wash. 7 × $3\frac{11}{16}$ (17.6 × 9.3). Ben. 1105. Metropolitan Museum of Art, New York. (Bequest of Mrs H. O. Havemeyer, 1929. H. O. Havemeyer Collection)
61 Rembrandt, *Death appearing to a Wedded Couple from an Open Grave*, 1639. Etching. 4 × 3 (10.9 × 7.8). B. 109. British Museum, London
62 Rembrandt, *The Unity of the Country* or *The Concord of State*, 1641. Panel. 29 × 39 (74 × 100). Br. 476. Museum Boymans–van Beuningen, Rotterdam
63 Rembrandt, *Copy After Raphael's 'Portrait of Baldassare Castiglione'*, 1639. Pen and brown ink with white body-colour. 6 × 8 (16.3 × 20.7). Ben. 451. Graphische Sammlung Albertina, Vienna
64 Govaert Flinck (1615–1660), *Portrait of Rembrandt* (detail), 1639. National Gallery, London
65 Balthasar van Berckenrode, *Map of Amsterdam* (detail), 1625. Engraving. British Museum, London
66 Reinier Nooms, called Zeeman, *St Anthoniespoort, Amsterdam*, 1636. Etching. 6 × 12 (15.5 × 30.5). British Museum, London
67 The front of Rembrandt's house in the St Anthoniesbreestraat, Amsterdam, today
68 The house in the Breestraat as it must have appeared when Rembrandt was living in it. Taken from F. Lugt, *Wandelingen met Rembrandt in en om Amsterdam*, Amsterdam, 1915
69 Titian (c. 1490–1576), *Portrait of a Man (formerly called Ariosto)*, c. 1512. Canvas. 32 × $26\frac{3}{4}$ (81.2 × 66.3). National Gallery, London
70 Rembrandt, *Self-portrait*, 1640. Canvas. 38 × 31 (97.5 × 79). Br. 34. National Gallery, London
71 Rembrandt, *Saskia's Bedroom*, c. 1639. Pen and brown ink with brown and grey wash, heightened with white. 6 × 7 (14.3 × 17.6). Ben. 426. Fondation Custodia (collection F. Lugt), Institut Néerlandais, Paris
72 Rembrandt, *Titia van Ulenborch*. Pen and brown wash. 7 × 6 (17.8 × 14.6). Ben. 441. Nationalmuseum, Stockholm
73 Rembrandt, *Saskia Ill*, c. 1642. Etching. $2\frac{3}{8}$ × 2 (6.1 × 5.1). B. 359. British Museum, London
74 Jacob van Meurs, *The Kloveniersdoelen, Amsterdam*. Engraved illustration to F. van Zesen, *Beschryving der Stadt Amsterdam*, Amsterdam, 1664. British Museum, London
75 Anon. Dutch draughtsman, *The House of Captain F. Banning Cocq on the Singel, Amsterdam*.

Drawing. Rijksmuseum, Amsterdam (De Graeff Album)
76 Bartholomeus van der Helst (1613?–1670), *The Company of Captain Roelof Bicker*, 1639. Canvas. $92\frac{1}{2}$ × $295\frac{1}{4}$ (235 × 750). Rijksmuseum, Amsterdam
77 Rembrandt, *The Parade of the Civic Guard under Captain F. Banning Cocq*, the so-called *Night Watch*, 1642. Canvas. 152 × 198 (387 × 502). Br. 410. Rijksmuseum, Amsterdam
78 Rembrandt, *Landscape with a Stone Bridge*, c. 1638. Panel. $7\frac{3}{4}$ × $11\frac{5}{8}$ (29.5 × 42.5). Br. 440. Rijksmuseum, Amsterdam
79 Rembrandt, *Winter Landscape*, 1646. Panel. $6\frac{11}{16}$ × $9\frac{1}{16}$ (17 × 23). Br. 452. Gemäldegalerie Alte Meister, Staatliche Kunstsammlungen Kassel
80 Rembrandt, *The Clump of Trees with a Vista*, 1652. Drypoint. $6\frac{3}{8}$ × 9 (15.6 × 21.1). B. 222, i. British Museum, London
81 Cornelis Danckerts, *Map of the Rijnland* (detail), 1647. Engraving. Leiden University (Bodel Nijenhuis Collection)
82 Rembrandt, *View of Amsterdam*, c. 1640. Etching. 4 × 6 (11.2 × 15.3). B. 210. British Museum, London
83 Rembrandt, *The Bulwark 'Het Blauwhoofd' on the West of Amsterdam*, c. 1641. Black chalk. 6 × 11 (16.6 × 27.5). Ben. 813. Museum Boymans van Beuningen, Rotterdam
84 Rembrandt, *View over the River Y from the Diemerdyke*, c. 1650. Pen and brown wash with white body-colour. 3 × 9 (7.6 × 24.4). Ben. 1239. Devonshire Collections, Chatsworth. Reproduced by permission of the Trustees of the Chatsworth Settlement
85 Rembrandt, *View of Diemen*, c. 1650. Pen and brown wash. 3 × 6 (8.8 × 15.5). B. 1231. Courtauld Institute Galleries, London (The Princes Gate Collection)
86 Rembrandt, *View of the River Amstel from the Blauwbrug, Amsterdam*, c. 1650. Pen and brown wash on vellum. 5 × 9 (13.2 × 23.2). Ben. 844. Rijksmuseum, Amsterdam
87 Rembrandt, *The Omval*, 1645. Etching and drypoint. 7 × 9 (18.5 × 22.5). B. 209. British Museum, London
88 Rembrandt, *The Bend in the River Amstel with the House of Kostverloren in the Trees*, c. 1650. Pen and brown and grey wash and white body-colour. 6 × 10 (13.6 × 25). Ben. 1265. Devonshire Collections, Chatsworth. Reproduced by permission of the Trustees of the Chatsworth Settlement
89 Rembrandt, *View of the Amstel with Amsterdam in the Background*, c. 1655. Pen and brown wash and

white body-colour. 6 × 11 (14.6 × 27.3). Ben. 1352. Kupferstichkabinett, Staatliche Museen zu Berlin

90 Rembrandt, *A Man Rowing a Boat on the Bullewyk*, c. 1650. Pen and brown wash and white body-colour. 5 × 8 (13.3 × 20.4). Ben. 1232. Devonshire Collections, Chatsworth. Reproduced by permission of the Trustees of the Chatsworth Settlement

91 Rembrandt, *View outside Haarlem*, traditionally known as *The Goldweigher's Field*, 1651. Etching and drypoint. 5 × 12 (12 × 31.9). B. 234. British Museum, London

92 Rembrandt, *The Western Gate at Rhenen*, c. 1648. Pen and brown wash. 6½ × 9 (16.5 × 22.6). Ben. 826. Teyler Museum, Haarlem

93 Jacob van der Ulft, *The New Town Hall and the Weighhouse, Amsterdam*. Etching. 16 × 21 (41.8 × 53.9). British Museum, London

94 Rembrandt, *The Old Town Hall of Amsterdam in Ruins*, 1652. Pen and brown ink and wash with red chalk. 6 × 8 (15 × 20.1). Ben. 1278. Rembrandthuis, Amsterdam

95 Reinier Nooms, called Zeeman, *The Montelbaarnstoren, Amsterdam*. Brush drawing in black ink. 5 × 10 (12.3 × 24.5). British Museum, London

96 Rembrandt, *The Montelbaarnstoren, Amsterdam*, c. 1652. Pen and brown wash. 6 × 6 (14.5 × 14.4). Ben. 1309. Rembrandthuis, Amsterdam

97 Rembrandt, *The Tower, Zwijgt-Utrecht, and the back of the Kloveniersdoelen, Amsterdam*, c. 1655. Pen and brown wash. 6 × 9 (16.4 × 23.5). Ben. 1334. Formerly Private Collection, Amsterdam. Photo Rijksmuseum, Amsterdam

98 Reinier Nooms, called Zeeman, *The Old Pesthuis outside Amsterdam*. Etching. 7 × 14 (19.2 × 34.6). British Museum, London

99 Rembrandt, *The Old Pesthuis or Fever Hospital outside Amsterdam*, c. 1655. Pen and brown ink. 5 × 10 (13.5 × 25). Ben. 1359. Formerly Private Collection, Amsterdam. Photo Rijksmuseum, Amsterdam

100 Rembrandt, *Holy Family in the Carpenter's Shop*, c. 1645. Pen and brown ink. 6⁵⁄₁₆ × 6¼ (16.1 × 15.8). Ben. 567. Musée Bonnat, Bayonne. Photo Lauros-Giraudon

101 Rembrandt, *Holy Family in the Carpenter's Shop*, 1645. Canvas. 46¹⁄₁₆ × 35¹³⁄₁₆ (117 × 91). Br. 570. Hermitage, Leningrad

102 Rembrandt, *Jacob and Esau*, c. 1648. Pen and ink with brown wash. 7⅞ × 6¹³⁄₁₆ (20 × 17.3). Ben. 606. British Museum, London

103 Rembrandt, *The Sacrifice of Isaac*, 1645. Etching. 6³⁄₁₆ × 5⅛ (15.7 × 13). B. 34. British Museum, London

104 Rembrandt, *The Hundred Guilder Print*, c. 1639–49. Etching and drypoint. 11 × 15¼ (27.8 × 38.8). B. 74, i. British Museum, London

105 Rembrandt, *Geertge Dircx(?)*, c. 1645. Pen and brown wash. 9 × 6 (22 × 15). Ben. 315. Teyler Museum, Haarlem

106 Rembrandt, *A Woman Bathing*, 1654. Oil on wood. 24 × 18 (61 × 46). Br. 437. National Gallery, London

107 Rembrandt, *Self-portrait holding his Palette, Brushes and Maulstick*, c. 1663. Canvas. 45 × 38 (114 × 97). Br. 52. The Greater London Council as Trustees of the Iveagh Bequest, Kenwood, London

108 Rembrandt, *Self-portrait*, 1658. Canvas. 52⅞ × 40⅞ (134 × 104). Br. 50. Copyright The Frick Collection, New York

109 Rembrandt, *Titus drawing at a Desk*, c. 1655. Pen and brush with brown wash. 7 × 5 (18.2 × 14). Ben. 1095. Kupferstichkabinett, Staatliche Kunstsammlungen, Dresden

110 Rembrandt, *Women sewing in the Artist's House*, c. 1655. Pen and brown wash. 5 × 8 (13.5 × 19.4). Ben. 1156. Statens Museum for Kunst, Copenhagen

111 Rembrandt, *Hendrickje (?) looking out of the Window*, c. 1655. Pen and brush with brown wash. 11 × 6¾ (29.2 × 16.2). Ben. 1099. Louvre, Paris (Rothschild Bequest)

112 Rembrandt, *Danaë*, 1636 and later. Canvas. 73 × 80 (185 × 203). Br. 474. Hermitage, Leningrad

113 Rembrandt, *Bathsheba at her Toilet*, 1654. Canvas. 56 × 56 (142 × 142). Br. 521. Louvre, Paris. Photo Lauros-Giraudon

114 Rembrandt, *Self-portrait*, 1652. Canvas. 45 × 32 (113 × 81). Br. 42. Kunsthistorisches Museum, Vienna

115 Rembrandt, *Self-portrait laughing*, c. 1668. Canvas. 32⁵⁄₁₆ × 24¹³⁄₁₆ (82 × 63). Br. 61. Wallraf Richartz-Museum, Cologne

116 Rembrandt, *A Model in the Artist's Studio*, c. 1655. Pen and grey wash, touched with white body-colour. 8 × 7 (20.5 × 19). Ben. 1161. Ashmolean Museum, Oxford

117 Rembrandt, *Naked Woman on a Mound*. Etching. 7 × 6⁵⁄₁₆ (17.7 × 16). B. 198, ii. British Museum, London

118 Rembrandt, *Reclining Female Nude*, c. 1646. Black chalk, heightened with white. 6½ × 10⁷⁄₁₆ (16.5 × 26.5). Ben. 712. Kunsthalle, Hamburg

119 Rembrandt, *Young Man seated, Another standing*, c. 1646. Etching. 7⅝ × 6 (19.4 × 12.8). B. 194, i. British Museum, London

120 Rembrandt, *Reclining Nude*, c. 1659. Pen and brush with brown wash, with some white body-

colour. $5\frac{5}{16}$ × $11\frac{1}{8}$ (13.5 × 28.3). Ben. 1137.
Rijksmuseum, Amsterdam

121 Rembrandt, *Woman at the Bath with a Hat beside her*, 1658. Etching and drypoint. $6\frac{1}{8}$ × 6 (15.6 × 12.9). B. 199, i. British Museum, London

122 Pupil of Rembrandt, *The Artist seated among his Pupils drawing from the Nude*. Pen and brown ink. Staatliche Kunstsammlungen, Weimar. Photo Louis Held

123 Rembrandt, *Satire on Art Criticism*, 1644. Pen and brown ink. 6 × 8 (15.6 × 20). Ben. A 35a. Private Collection

124 Rembrandt, *The Adoration of the Shepherds*, 1646. Canvas. 38 × 28 (98 × 72). Ben. 574. Alte Pinakothek, Munich

125 Rembrandt, *Jan Six*, 1647. Etching. 10 × 7 (24.5 × 19.1). B. 285, ii. British Museum, London

126 Rembrandt, *Medea, or the Marriage of Jason and Creusa*, 1648. Etching and drypoint. 9 × 7 (24 × 17.7). B. 112, iii. British Museum, London

127 Rembrandt, *Jan Six writing at his Estate at Ijmond(?)*, *c.* 1655. Pen and brown wash. 5 × 8 (13.7 × 19.7). Ben. 1172. Louvre, Paris. Photo Giraudon

128 Rembrandt, *St John the Baptist preaching*, *c.* 1655. Pen and brown wash with touches of white body-colour. 6 × 8 (14.5 × 20.4). Ben. 969. Louvre, Paris

129 Anon. 19th-century etching after Rembrandt, *Jan Six*. $20\frac{1}{4}$ × $17\frac{3}{4}$ (51.5 × 45). British Museum, London

130 Rembrandt, *Aristotle contemplating the Bust of Homer*, 1653. Canvas. 55 × 52 (139 × 133). Br. 478. The Metropolitan Museum of Art, New York. (Purchased with special funds and gifts of friends of the Museum, 1961)

131 Rembrandt, *Ephraim Bonus*, 1647. Etching and drypoint. 10 × 7 (24 × 17.7). B. 74, i. British Museum, London

132 Rembrandt, *Arnold Tholinx*, *c.* 1656. Etching and drypoint. 8 × 6 (19.8 × 14.9). B. 284, i. British Museum, London

133 Rembrandt, *Jan Asselyn*, *c.* 1647. Etching and drypoint. 8 × 7 (21.5 × 17). B. 277, i. British Museum, London

134 Rembrandt, *Clement de Jonghe*, 1651. Etching and drypoint. 8 × 6 (20.6 × 16.1). B. 272, iv. British Museum, London

135 Rembrandt, *Jan Lutma the Elder*, 1656. Etching and drypoint. 8 × 6 (19.7 × 14.8). B. 276, ii. British Museum, London

136 Rembrandt, *The Anatomy Lesson of Dr Johan Deyman*, 1656. Canvas. 39 × 52 (100 × 132). Br. 414. Rijksmuseum, Amsterdam

137 Rembrandt, *The Skeleton Rider*, *c.* 1655. Pen and

brown ink. 6 × 6 (15.3 × 14.8). Ben. 728. Hessisches Landesmuseum, Darmstadt

138 Rembrandt, *The Anatomy Lesson of Dr Johan Deyman*, *c.* 1656. Pen and brown ink. 4 × 5 (11 × 13.3). Ben. 1175. Rijksmuseum, Amsterdam

139 Rembrandt, *St Jerome in an Italian Landscape*, *c.* 1653. Etching and drypoint. $10\frac{3}{16}$ × $8\frac{1}{4}$ (25.9 × 21). B. 104, i. British Museum, London

140 Rembrandt, *The Prophet Elisha with the Widow and her Sons*, *c.* 1657. Pen and brown ink. $6\frac{3}{4}$ × 10 (17.2 × 25.4). Ben. 1027. Museum of Fine Arts, Boston. (Ernest W. Longfellow Fund: Charles H. Bayley Picture and Painting Fund. Jessie H. Wilkinson Fund)

141 Rembrandt, *Christ appearing to the Apostles*, 1656. Etching. $6\frac{3}{8}$ × $8\frac{1}{4}$ (16.2 × 21). B. 89. British Museum, London

142 Rembrandt, *Christ taken Prisoner*, *c.* 1656. Pen and ink with brown wash. $6\frac{7}{8}$ × $10\frac{1}{4}$ (17.5 × 26). Ben. 1022. Courtauld Institute Galleries, London (The Princes Gate Collection)

143 Rembrandt, *Nathan admonishing David*, *c.* 1655. Pen and ink with brown wash, heightened with white. $7\frac{3}{16}$ × 10 (18.3 × 25.2). Ben. 948. Metropolitan Museum of Art, New York. (Bequest of Mrs H. O. Havemeyer, 1929. The H. O. Havemeyer Collection

144 Anon. Dutch draughtsman, *The Keizerskroon Inn in the Calverstraat, Amsterdam*. Drawing. Municipal Archives, Amsterdam

145 Rembrandt, *Four Orientals under a Tree*, *c.* 1656. Pen and ink with brown wash on Japanese paper. $7\frac{5}{8}$ × 5 (19.4 × 12.5). Ben. 1187. British Museum, London

146 Rembrandt, *Abraham entertaining the Angels*, 1656. Etching and drypoint. $6\frac{1}{4}$ × $5\frac{3}{16}$ (15.9 × 13.1). B. 29. British Museum, London

147 Rembrandt, *Lot and his Daughters*, *c.* 1656. Pen and brown ink. $3\frac{7}{8}$ × $6\frac{7}{16}$ (9.9 × 16.4). Ben. 1006. Courtauld Institute Galleries, London (The Princes Gate Collection)

148 Rembrandt, *Self-portrait*, 1657. Canvas. 21 × 17 (53 × 43.5). Br. 48. Duke of Sutherland Collection, on loan to the National Gallery of Scotland, Edinburgh. Photo Annan, Glasgow

149 Bill announcing the sale of Rembrandt's collection to be held at the Keizerskroon in the Calverstraat, Amsterdam. 1658. British Museum, London

150 Rembrandt, *Abraham Francen*, *c.* 1656. Etching and drypoint. 6 × 8 (15.2 × 20.8). B. 273, i. British Museum, London

151 Rembrandt, *Thomas Jacobsz. Haringh*, *c.* 1656. Etching and drypoint. 8 × 6 (19.5 × 14.9). B. 274, ii. British Museum, London

152 Anon. follower of Rembrandt, *The Entrance Hall of the Artist's House on the Rozengracht, Amsterdam.* Pen and brown wash. $6\frac{3}{8} \times 6$ (16.2 × 15.2). British Museum, London

153 Rembrandt, *Titus, c.* 1655. Canvas. $30\frac{1}{4} \times 24\frac{3}{4}$ (77 × 63). B. 120. Museum Boymans–van Beuningen, Rotterdam

154 Rembrandt, *Hendrickje Stoffels* (detail), 1660. Canvas. 30 × 26 (76 × 67). Br. 118. The Metropolitan Museum of Art, New York (Gift of Archer M. Huntington, in memory of his father, Collis Potter Huntington, 1926)

155 Rembrandt, *Lieven Willemsz. van Coppenol with his Grandson, c.* 1658. Etching and drypoint. 10 × 7 (25.7 × 18.9). B. 282, iv. British Museum, London

156 Rembrandt, *Gérard de Lairesse,* 1665. Canvas. 44 × 34 (112 × 87). Br. 321. Metropolitan Museum of Art, New York, Robert Lehman Collection

157 Rembrandt, *Jeremias de Decker,* 1666. Panel. 28 × 22 (71 × 56). Br. 320. Hermitage, Leningrad

158 Govaert Flinck (1615–1660), *The Conspiracy of Julius Civilis, c.* 1659. Black lead and brown wash. $6\frac{9}{16} \times 6\frac{11}{16}$ (16.6 × 17). Kunsthalle, Hamburg

159 Rembrandt, *The Conspiracy of Julius Civilis, c.* 1661. Pen and ink with brown wash, with some white body-colour. $7\frac{11}{16} \times 8$ (19.6 × 18). Ben. 1061. Staatliche Graphische Sammlung, Munich

160 Rembrandt, *The Portrait of the Syndics of the Clothmakers' Guild,* 1662. Canvas. 75 × 110 (191.5 × 279). Br. 415. Rijksmuseum, Amsterdam

161 Rembrandt, *Homer dictating to a Scribe, c.* 1663. Pen and brush with brown wash, heightened with white. $5\frac{11}{16} \times 6\frac{9}{16}$ (14.5 × 16.7). Ben. 1066. Nationalmuseum, Stockholm

162 Rembrandt, *Homer,* 1663. Canvas. $42\frac{1}{2} \times 32\frac{1}{2}$ (108 × 82.5). Br. 483. Mauritshuis, The Hague

163 Rembrandt, *The Conspiracy of Julius Civilis,* 1661. Canvas. 77 × 122 (196 × 309). Br. 482. Nationalmuseum, Stockholm

164 Rembrandt, *Self-portrait as St Paul,* 1661. Canvas. 38 × 30 (91 × 76). Br. 59. Rijksmuseum, Amsterdam

165 Rembrandt, *The Jewish Bride, c.* 1668. Canvas. 48 × 65 (121.5 × 166.5). Br. 416. Rijksmuseum, Amsterdam

166 Rembrandt's and Titus's signatures on a document dated 3 June 1665 in the State Archives in The Hague

167 Titus van Rijn, *Meleager and Atalanta.* Pen and brown wash. 8 × 8 (19.4 × 19.4). Private Collection, London

168 Rembrandt, *Self-portrait,* 1669. Canvas. $33\frac{7}{8} \times 27\frac{3}{4}$ (86 × 70.5). Br. 55. National Gallery, London

169 F. de Wit, *The Westerkerk, Amsterdam.* Etching. 5 × 5 (13 × 13). British Museum, London

170 Notice of Rembrandt's burial in the Westerkerk, Amsterdam, 8 October 1669. Archives of the Reformed Church of Amsterdam

# Select bibliography

This has been confined to books in English.

**Monographs:** J. Rosenberg, *Rembrandt: Life and Work* (2nd ed., 1964): although out of date in certain respects, still retains sterling qualities as an interpretation; B. Haak, *Rembrandt: His life, His Work, His Time* (1969): detailed account of life and background with excellent illustrations.

**Life:** W. Strauss and M. van der Meulen, *The Rembrandt Documents* (New York, 1979), transcribed and translated into English, incorporating recent archival research by such Dutch scholars as I. H. van Eeghen, H. F. Wijnman and S. Dudok van Heel.

**Paintings:** A. Bredius, *The Complete Edition of the Paintings of Rembrandt*, revised ed. by H. Gerson (1969): concise scholarly comments on each picture included in the original edition with execrable plates; H. Gerson, *Rembrandt Paintings* (Amsterdam, London and New York, 1968): detailed study of the paintings accepted by the author with good illustrations; Rembrandt Research Project, *A Corpus of Rembrandt Paintings*, I (The Hague, Boston and London, 1982): only covering the Leiden years, this is the first in a projected series of exhaustive catalogues of the paintings; M. Kitson, *Rembrandt* (Oxford, 1982): excellent short study of Rembrandt as a painter.

**Drawings:** O. Benesch, *The Drawings of Rembrandt*, 6 vols (1973): the standard *catalogue raisonné*, although the first edition (1954–7) has better illustrations; S. Slive, *Drawings of Rembrandt with a Selection of Drawings by His Pupils and Followers*, 2 vols (New York, 1965): based on a facsimile series published between 1888 and 1911, with pertinent comments on each drawing; O. Benesch, *Rembrandt as a Draughtsman* (1960); C. White, *The Drawings of Rembrandt* (The British Museum, 1962); B. Haak, *Rembrandt Drawings* (1974): the last three items contain essays.

**Etchings:** L. Münz, *Rembrandt's Etchings*, 2 vols (1952): a *catalogue raisonné* with a lengthy introduction; C. White, *Rembrandt as an Etcher: A study of the artist at work*, 2 vols (1969); C. White and K. Boon, *Rembrandt's Etchings: an illustrated critical catalogue*, 2 vols (Amsterdam, 1969); *Rembrandt: All the etchings reproduced in true size* (Maarssen, 1977): excellent illustrations.

**Special studies:** S. Slive, *Rembrandt and his Critics 1630–1730* (The Hague, 1953); W. Heckscher, *Rembrandt's Anatomy of Dr Nicolaas Tulp: an Iconological Study* (New York, 1958); H. Gerson, *Seven Letters by Rembrandt* (The Hague, 1961); K. Clark, *Rembrandt and the Italian Renaissance* (1966); J. Held, *Rembrandt's Aristotle and Other Rembrandt Studies* (1969); R. Fuchs, *Rembrandt in Amsterdam* (New York, 1969); H.-M. Rotermund, *Rembrandt's Drawings and Etchings for the Bible* (Philadelphia and Boston, 1969); H. van de Waal, *Steps towards Rembrandt* (Amsterdam and London, 1974): includes essays on chiaroscuro, the *Julius Civilis*, Rembrandt and the theatre, and the *Syndics*; C. Wright, *Rembrandt: Self-portraits* (1982); E. Haverkamp-Begemann, *Rembrandt: The Nightwatch* (Princeton, 1982); W. Schupbach, *The Paradox of Rembrandt's 'Anatomy of Dr. Tulp'* (1982).

## FURTHER BIBLIOGRAPHY

Apart from the above, a number of more specialized works were consulted in preparing this book.

**General:** The supplementary notes by H. Wijnman to my *Rembrandt: biographie in woord en beeld* (The Hague, 1964).

**Chapter One:** For Rembrandt and Lastman, see W. Stechow, *Oud Holland*, LXXXIV (1969), 148–62; for Lievens, see Herzog Anton Ulrich-Museum, Brunswick, *Jan Lievens ein Maler im Schatten Rembrandts* (1979).

**Chapter Two:** For Rembrandt and England, see the present writer, *Apollo*, LXXVI (1962), 177–84; for the identification of the sitters in *The Shipbuilder and his Wife*, see I. H. van Eeghen, *Maandblad Amstelodamum*, LVII (1970), 121–7.

**Chapter Three:** For Rembrandt and Titian's *'Ariosto'*, see E. de Jongh, *Delta* (Summer 1969), 49–67, and C. Brown, *Second Sight* (National Gallery, 1980); for the identification of the landscapes, see F. Lugt, *Mit Rembrandt in Amsterdam* (Berlin, 1920).

**Chapter Four:** For an interpretation of the *Self-portrait laughing*, see A. Blankert in *Album Amicorum J. G. van Gelder* (The Hague, 1973), 32–9; for

Bathsheba, see H. Bramsen, *Burlington Magazine*, XCII (1950), 128–31; for Rembrandt's teaching, see E. Haverkamp-Begemann in The Art Institute of Chicago, *Rembrandt after Three Hundred Years* (1969), 21–30, and J. Emmens, *Rembrandt en de regels van de kunst* (Utrecht, 1968); for Rembrandt and Six, see C. Bille, *Apollo*, LXXXV (1967), 160–65; for the drawing of Anna Wijmer, see E. Haverkamp-Begemann in *Studies in Western Art* (Princeton, 1963), 59–65.

**Chapter Five:** For Rembrandt's financial problems, see J. F. Backer, *Gazette des Beaux-Arts*,

LXVI (1924), no. 9, 238–48, no. 10, 219–40, 361–8, LXVII (1925), no. 11, 50–60; for an interpretation of Rembrandt's collection, see R. Scheller, *Oud Holland*, LXXIV (1969), 1–81; for the Guild of St Luke, see I. H. van Eeghen, *Jaarboek Amstelodamum*, LXI (1969), 65–103; for the X-rays of the *Syndics*, see A. van Schendel, *Oud Holland*, LXXI (1956), 1–23; for Rembrandt's religious iconography, see J. Bialostocki, *Münchner Jahrbuch der bildenden Kunst*, VIII (1957), 195–210, C. Tümpel, *Jahrbuch der Hamburger Kunstsammlungen*, XIII (1968), 95–126, and ibid, *Nederlands Kunsthistorisch Jaarboek*, XX (1969), 107–98.

# Index

*Numbers in italics refer to the illustrations*